CH00545924

A FORGOTTEN NORWICH ARTIST

Further details of Poppyland Publishing titles can be found at
www.poppyland.co.uk

Join us for more Norfolk and Suffolk stories and background at
www.facebook.com/poppylandpublishing

Catherine Maude Nichols (1847–1923) in the early 1900s.

A forgotten Norwich artist

Catherine Maude Nichols, 1847–1923

by

Pamela Inder

&

Marion Aldis

POPPYLAND
PUBLISHING

Copyright © 2015

First published 2015 by Poppyland Publishing, Cromer, NR27 9AN
www.poppyland.co.uk

ISBN 978-1-909796-20-1

All rights reserved. No part of this publication may be reproduced, stored in a retrieval system
or transmitted by any means, mechanical, photocopying, recording or otherwise, without the
written permission of the publishers.

Designed and typeset in 10.5 on 13.5 pt Gilgamesh by Watermark, NR27 9ER
Printed by ImprintDigital

Picture credits
*Images are reproduced by courtesy of the following (numbers are picture numbers, not page
   numbers):*

British Museum: 5, 27, 31, 39, 40, 46
The Carrara family (photo by Shelly Malcolm): 95
Sarah Colegrave Fine Art: 28, 29, 35
Mr and Mrs M Emery: 43, 44, 45
Martin Laurance: 36, 37
Norfolk County Council Library and Information Service: 4, 11, 32, 33, 34, 38, 51, 59, 83, 90, 94,
   96; Picture Norfolk 7, 8, 12, 91, 97, 98
Norfolk Record Office: 3, 15, 16, 20, 21, 58, 60, 61, 62, 63, 64, 65, 67, 68, 69, 70, 84, 86, 87, 88,
   89, 92, 93, 100
Norwich Museums and Archaeology Service, Norwich Castle Museum and Art Gallery: front
   cover, frontispiece, 18a & b, 19, 22, 26, 30, 41, 66, 85, 71, 72, 115
The Order of Bards and Druids and Philip Carr-Gomm: 14
Personalia: 9
St John's Cathedral, Norwich: 48
Shrewsbury School: 13
Evelyn Simak, Creative Commons: 6

The following plates come from:
The Great Gothic Fane: 50, 52, 53, 55, 56, 57, 101
The Maddermarket Theatre, Norwich by Andrew Stephenson: 49
warhorseandworldwar1@weebly.com: 99

Foreword

I first met Pamela Inder and Marion Aldis when we got together in Norwich to share our mutual fascination for the subject of this book, Catherine Maude Nichols. I've studied the life of this elusive woman, and written about her, for some years. It soon became apparent I had not been ploughing a lone furrow, and that in planning a book about her, Pamela and Marion had dug much deeper than I had.

Their work has reaped rewards. This book puts Nichols into context and character. She was a woman of the nineteenth century, who lived well into the twentieth. A female artist, she achieved commercial success in a male-dominated world. Nichols was a person of such contrariness that she was able to love Norwich as an inspiration, but berate it as a city. These are just some of the facets of her that you will find explored and detailed in this fascinating account.

Catherine Maude Nichols is in many ways an enigma. Her life is full of contradictions and unanswered questions. In truth she has not helped the historian. Much of what she said in interviews and articles adds to the mystery rather than clarifies it. An efficient and assiduous self-publicist, she also frequently drew a veil when it suited her. She was not averse either it seems to embroidering stories and even changing 'facts'.

All of this means greater credit is due to Pamela Inder and Marion Aldis for their detective work in bringing together what I believe is the most complete picture we have to date of this extraordinary woman.

Pete Goodrum
Writer and Broadcaster
Norwich
July 2014

Acknowledgements

We would like to thank the following individuals and institutions who have, in various ways, helped us with our research: Maddie Bartle, the Carrara family, Mr and Mrs M. Emery, Pete Goodrum, Stephen Slack, the staffs of the Millennium Library, Norwich, Norwich Record Office and the Print Room at the British Museum, Giorgia Bottinelli and Francesca Vanke of Norwich Castle Museum, Caroline Palmer at the Ashmolean Museum, Michael Bishop of Personalia, Sarah Colegrave Fine Art and Mick Morrogh at Shrewsbury School.

Contents

List of Illustrations

Notes on money

It is never possible to be entirely accurate when converting historical prices to their modern equivalents. The figures below are based on the conversion tables provided by the National Archives and give some idea of the changing value in modern (2005) purchasing power of £10 at various points in Catherine Maude Nichols' lifetime and they give some idea of what she was charging for her work.

1850	£585.30
1860	£431.60
1870	£457.00
1880	£483.10
1890	£598.90
1900	£570.60
1910	£570.60
1915	£430.60
1920	£212.10

Throughout the period in question, the pound (£) was divided into 20 shillings (s), each containing 12 pence (d); the guinea was 21 shillings, so half a guinea was 10s 6d — art works often being priced in guineas.

1. Carlton Terrace, Surrey Street.
Kate Nichols moved to number 73, c.1900.

2. Kate Nichols' front door.

I

17th February 1908

73 Surrey Street, Norwich

It had been a most successful afternoon, Kate thought. Alastor had looked simply splendid, so tall and brown in those beautiful white robes with that wonderful glittering Indian stole draped over one shoulder. All her guests had seemed to enjoy themselves. Of course, there were some people who disapproved of Alastor — 'dabbling in the occult' they called his prophecies. But a truly artistic temperament gave one insight, opened the mind, enabled one to accept that there were things that could not be explained by faith alone. She had discussed this matter many times with her good friend, Mrs Pym, and they were in perfect agreement. Dear Alastor, such a find! So gifted! And so sad that he was all alone in the world — widowed many years ago, he had told her — but he was too fine of feeling, too sensitive, to have told her anything about his late wife. She did not even know the poor woman's name. Kate understood what it was like to be alone, to mourn a lost love. Perhaps she could give him a little treat, take him on holiday with her, to Cromer perhaps. The sea air would do them both good, they could get to know each other better. . . . She stopped herself. What nonsense for a woman of sixty to be thinking!

On the train from Norwich to Eccles Road

Berthalina Mann chattered excitedly. Alastor the Palmist was so handsome, almost regal. Had her mother noticed his beautiful hands, so slim, so perfectly manicured? Had she seen that huge ring with the mysterious symbols? Berthalina was sure that he had second sight, he'd told her things about herself that no stranger could possibly have known.

Mary Mann knew better than to interrupt her daughter in mid-flow but she was only half-listening to her. Poor dear Bertie, thirty-five and still so susceptible to a handsome face! She herself had been unimpressed by Kate's newest protégé,

the latest in a long line of lame ducks; he'd take
advantage of Kate's generosity in the end, they
always did. However did Kate square this new-
found belief in palmistry and astrology with her
devotion to the Catholic Church? She was prone
to extravagant enthusiasms, always had been,
ever since they were girls at school together. And
these days she was quite short of money, poor dear,
having given so much of her inheritance away to
help waifs and strays — both animal and human.
Maybe Mary Mann could commission a miniature
of herself — or Bertie — to help Kate a little? She was
quite well off at present, thanks to Mr Methuen.
Two books published last year, two to come out this
year. And clever Mr Watt was now insisting that she
accept no less than £3 per 1,000 words for her short
stories. Come to think of it, Kate's relationship
with Alastor would make a wonderful subject for a
short story! What should she call him? The Great
— what? Something foreign-sounding? How about
'Cavassa'? And Kate Nichols? Judy, perhaps — yes,
'Judy Harrison, beauty lover'. An idea began to
form in Mary Mann's fertile brain.

3. *Berthalina Mann, who attended
Kate's tea party on 17th February
1908.*

21, Southwell Road, Norwich

Alastor the Palmist let himself in through the front door. 'That you, William?'
called his wife. 'Did the tea party go well?'

'I believe so, my dear,' he replied. 'I believe so. This really could be the making
of us, you know. Grand ladies are as anxious to hear good news as anyone else.
It's like my Aunt Susannah always used to say "Watch and listen. They'll show
you what they want you to tell them." But you should have seen them, such a
collection of queer old sticks — all that black silk and lace and haughtiness.'

'As you well know, I am unlikely ever to see them,' said his wife, rather sharply.
'Since you are determined to tell everyone I am dead and to pretend that
Susannah and Maud never existed.'

'Just play-acting, my dear,' William Smith answered soothingly. 'It's better for
business if the clients think I am to be pitied. You know that. We've talked about
it many times. It means nothing.'

And with that, Maria Smith had to be content.

****

Obviously we cannot really know what people said and thought on that February evening over a century ago. But the scenarios outlined above are based on hard fact. Kate Nichols did invite friends to a tea party to meet Alastor the Palmist on 17th February 1908. She and her close friend, Mrs Radford Pym, were involved with Alastor for at least two years and they invited him to a series of events. Kate did spend a holiday with him in July 1908, though we don't know where, and her friends, according to Berthalina Mann's diary, were 'most facetious' about it — perhaps they suspected that Kate really did feel more than friendship for the handsome astrologer.[1] Mrs Pym invited him to stay with her in her holiday cottage in Sheringham for a week in August the following year. Mrs Pym's companion, Lilly Bull, described her employer as 'too open minded' to care what the narrowly religious thought about palmistry and astrology, and Kate probably followed Mrs Pym's lead in this as she did in so many things. However, even Mrs Pym was a little thrown when her friend Father Ignatius, a Norwich eccentric who set up his own religious brotherhood in 1870 on Elm Hill (thus sparking a series of riots), invited himself to Sheringham for the same week that Alastor was to be with her. Fortunately Mrs Pym owned the cottage next door to her own and installed Alastor there for the duration. The two men took their meals with her, but in different rooms at different times — and somehow the subterfuge worked.[2]

Mary Elizabeth Mann (Polly to her friends and family) was one of the guests at the tea party in February, as was her artist daughter, Berthalina, always known as 'Bertie'. Bertie recorded her impressions of Alastor and her initial enthusiasm for him in her diary, and it is clear from the same diary that she was, indeed, highly susceptible to male beauty. She writes of four meetings with Alastor, and by the final one she had become disillusioned and decided he was a complete fraud — but still she wrote: 'I think personal beauty is the most wonderful of all the gifts of the gods. Here is this man, who in himself is quite third rate — a charlatan by trade . . . yet there he stood — a king before his subjects — by the divine right of personal beauty. And I, who quite saw through the careful arrangement of the dramatic entry, nonetheless took him a cup of tea.'

Polly Mann (née Rackham) and Kate Nichols had been at Mrs Dunnett's school together as young teenagers. Polly married a farmer, Fairman Joseph Mann, and they lived at Manor Farm in Shropham, just three miles from Eccles Road station, and the family often travelled to and from Norwich by train. Polly — writing as Mary E. Mann — was a well-known novelist, and between 1883 and 1919 she produced 33 novels, six collections of short stories, and several hundred short stories for magazines. 'The Eerie', based on Kate's relationship with Alastor, was first published in *Cassell's Magazine* in January 1909, and was included in the collection *Bound Together* in 1910. In 1908 Mary Mann was working for Methuen and her agent was A. P. Watt. In a letter to her nephew in 1908 she talks of commissioning a miniature from Kate Nichols because she wants to help her out financially — though we do not know whether the order was ever placed.[3]

'Alastor the Palmist' was born William Robert Wilson Smith in 1857, in Norwich. He was a shoemaker's son, and at the time of the 1881 census he and his wife and their first child were living with his widowed aunt, Susannah Smith, in Lakenham. She described herself as an 'astrologer', a trade she seems to have taken up after the death of her leather worker husband, John. William is described as a 'trainee astrologer'. He had married Maria Hudson in 1878 and in time they had two daughters, Susannah and Maud. The census shows us that the couple were still living together on Southwell Road in 1911, in what had been William's aunt's house, with their eldest daughter Susannah, her husband, Robert Till, and her baby daughter, their grandchild, little Olivia.

We know from Bertie Mann's diaries that Kate and her friends believed 'Alastor' to be a widower. She also tells us that he sometimes worked as an artist's model — William Smith's handsome face was his fortune in more ways than one. It seems that around the time Kate and Mrs Pym got to know him, '"the palmist mystic" had for a season been exciting great interest at an exhibition in Norwich'.[4] There are comparatively few other references to him, but in October 1908 we know he performed at a garden party at Sefton Park in Buckinghamshire, held by Lord and Lady Decles in aid of Our Dumb Friends' League, wearing the 'white robes and oriental draperies' that we say he wore at Kate Nichols' tea party. The League was particularly concerned with the ill-treatment of horses by carriers and tradesmen and funded a fleet of 'horse ambulances' to rescue injured and dying animals.[5] This was a cause dear to Kate Nichols' heart and it is probable that she secured the booking for Alastor.

Maria Smith died in 1914, and some time after that William seems to have gone out to India to entertain the troops — there are references in the press to 'Alastor, the well-known astrologer' entertaining airmen at Sibi in Baluchistan in July, 1922, for example.[6] He seems to have died in India.

We do not know whether he did take advantage of Kate Nichols' generosity,[7] nor do we know how, or exactly when, their relationship came to an end. Of itself, their friendship does not form a major part of Catherine Maude Nichols' life, but it is a colourful episode, at odds with some of the things we know about her and totally in keeping with others. She was, as we shall see, a complicated, contradictory character.

2

Timeline

In many ways Catherine Maude Nichols is a biographer's nightmare. She was very conscious of her public image and she carefully manipulated the facts to ensure that we only know what she wanted us to know. She left behind her a considerable body of work, but very little that tells us anything about the progress of her career and almost nothing that tells us about her as a person.

In the absence of letters or diaries we can only reconstruct Kate's career from dated works, odd documents and details of exhibitions. We know she travelled around the UK and that there were visits to the Continent, but we cannot date them precisely. There is a further problem here in that those of her etchings that bear dates are likely to be dated the year they were *etched* rather than the year in which the drawing on which they were based was made — and turning her sketches into etchings would have had to wait until she got back to Norwich to her studio and her tools. Her oil paintings may well also have been worked up back home from sketches and notes made in the field. From the evidence of works in public collections and ones that have been advertised for sale online, we know that she visited Bristol, London and Workington in Cumbria as well as France, Jersey, Germany and Cornwall. She also told the author of *Cox's Who's Who in Norfolk and Suffolk* that she had travelled in Switzerland, and a single sketch of Bruges in Norwich Castle Museum tells us she may have visited Belgium. However, the fact that the vast majority of her traceable work is of Norwich and Norfolk rather than these other places would suggest that her trips away from the county were relatively brief.

Apparently she told friends that she started drawing as a little girl of about six, sketching flowers and leaves and using her father's medical skeleton as a model.[1] But most children draw. Indeed, at six she was an only child with busy parents; drawing and painting — and reading and writing stories — probably occupied a good deal of her time. In Kate's childhood children were expected to be seen and not heard, and drawing is a quiet, sedentary, lady-like occupation. True, not all little girls would have had a skeleton as a model — but not all little girls had fathers who were doctors.

We don't know when she left school, but it was probably somewhere between 1863 and 1865. Mrs Dunnett's older pupils only seem to have gone to school for occasional lessons rather than putting in full time attendance — certainly Polly Rackham seems to have done this and it is quite possible that Kate did, too. A number of letters from, and about, Kate survive in the Mann collection; none of them makes any mention of her talent for sketching — but her friends may have been so aware of her artistic ambitions that they saw no reason to mention them.[2] Another possibility is that in the late 1860s/early 1870s Kate was trying to fulfil her parents' expectations and find a husband. It may be cynical to say so, but she may not have become so totally dedicated to her art until she was reasonably sure that she was not going to marry.

She must have visited France in or around 1876–77 as the first picture she exhibited at a Royal Academy Summer Exhibition was of Normandy and it was hung in 1877, the year Kate was thirty. Of course she may have submitted works previously but not have had them selected — we have no way of knowing — but she does tell us that that picture was the first ever etching she made.[3] Given her ability to bend the facts this may not be entirely true (her first known dated etching is labelled 1875), but it does suggest that it was an early work. The pictures she submitted in 1877 and 1878 were both dry-points, a technique she probably learnt at the School of Art. Prints were less highly regarded than paintings; they were seen as a way of reproducing works of art rather than as art-works in their own right; the Royal Society of Painter-Etchers was founded specifically to dispel the idea that engravings were in some way inferior to paintings. Nonetheless, if Kate's father

4. *Catherine Maude Nichols.*
Source unknown.

championed her career as enthusiastically as she later claimed, he must have been delighted to know, shortly before he died, that his daughter's work had been exhibited at the Academy.

With Dr Nichols' death, Kate became a woman of means. She had £1,000 that was hers to spend as she wished — 'for her own absolute use' in Dr Nichol's words[4] — and she had the expectation of an even larger sum to come in the future when her mother died and her father's estate was divided between her and her siblings. No doubt her father expected her to continue living at home with her mother paying all the bills, and under those circumstances he had provided for her handsomely. But he reckoned without her conversion to Catholicism. As we shall see, she was baptised into the Catholic Church in 1882. It seems this may have caused a rift and at some point Kate moved out of the family home. In 1891 she was in lodgings a few doors away, at 12 Surrey Street, with Amelia Rudd and her family, and by 1900 she had moved into a house of her own, 73 Carlton Terrace, at the far end of Surrey Street, opposite the convent.

Living independently was obviously more expensive than living at home, but we really know very little about Kate's financial position. It may be that she had other money of her own that had been settled on her before her father's death, or that she still had some sort of allowance from his estate — he had been a wealthy man. Part of the image she liked to present to the world was that she was a struggling artist, bravely making ends meet — but in reality she could afford to live in a large, comfortable house, she employed a servant, travelled, was known for her generous donations to charity and hobnobbed with the rich and famous. She could afford to have her books privately printed, she must have financed her one-woman shows and she paid to ship work to exhibitions abroad. Sales of her work may have eventually covered the cost of these ventures but the money for them had to be found up front. Compared to her friend, Mrs Radford Pym, Kate Nichols was not a rich woman, but she was certainly not poor. It is also hard to know how much of her income came from her work because, though we know what she charged, we do not know how much she sold. For a folder of four etchings produced to commemorate George Borrow in 1913, for example, she charged two guineas — four guineas for signed editions — and the print run was 350.[5] A catalogue survives of an exhibition she held at the Queen's Hotel in Manchester. It is undated so we do not know when the exhibition took place, but she was charging between three and eight guineas for her oil paintings, according to size, and ten guineas or more for her watercolours. Sketches and engravings were priced at between two and a half and ten guineas.[6] These were not extortionate sums, but an artist who was truly struggling would not have been able to command even these prices.

The Norwich Art Circle was formed in 1885 and Kate exhibited with them almost every year. Most of their catalogues contain prices and we can see that though for the most part Kate's prices were modest, as time went by they did increase. Clearly there were some works which she felt were exceptional and could command a high price. In October 1915, for example, she was charging £42 for an oil painting called 'Summer' and £21 apiece for two pictures of fir trees. Of course, during and immediately after the war there was rampant inflation and Kate was sufficient of a businesswoman to raise her prices in line with the market. The value of money halved (see 'Notes on Money' on p. 11) and by the end of her life her average asking prices had more than doubled from those she was asking in Manchester.

We do know Kate Nichols was a prolific artist and exhibitor, producing dry-points, etchings and lithographs, sketches in pencil and ink, paintings in watercolour and oils, book plates and miniatures, but while various dictionaries of artists give lists of places where she exhibited and numbers of works, we seldom know when those exhibitions took place or what she showed. Her exhibits at the Royal Academy and the Royal Society of Painter-Etchers are well documented, but she also showed works at numerous other galleries and in her own interviews she talks of sending works to exhibitions in Paris, Munich, Venice, Melbourne and St Louis.[7] We also know she held a number of one woman shows in London, Manchester and Norwich. In addition to her artwork, she wrote poetry, stories, essays and novels and produced lavishly illustrated books. She was dedicated and industrious.

But what we also know about Catherine Maude Nichols is that she had a strong sense of her own importance and a tendency to exaggerate. She saved favourable notices of her work and published them in hand-outs and on the cover of folders of her etchings. She gave numerous interviews in the press and to all sorts of magazines, from the *Women's Penny Paper* to *The Bookman*, and she comes over as self-confident and proud of her achievements.

She was eccentric, hardworking, talented and opinionated, a feminist who had no desire to fight for women's rights. 'While men have all the power they make laws in their own favour, I feel that. Still, I think men and women have different parts to play in the world only you cannot draw a hard and fast line' she told the readers of the *Women's Penny Paper*.[8] 'I went into a shop the other day where they sell nothing but little falals for ladies, veils and lace edgings and ribbons; and was waited on by three broad-shouldered young men. It was ridiculous. I thought they were out of their "sphere!" It is certainly a good thing if women's interests should be looked after, but I do not feel I can take up that subject.' Later writers speak of her 'salt of a bright twinkling humour', of the wonderful parties she hosted, of her generosity and her ability to make people feel that they mattered — 'I do not remember any unkindness. Always there was the same interest and sympathy. No-one — nothing was too little for her individual attention.'⁹ Yet her written work is sombre, full of references to lost love and hopes for a better life in the world to come; there is little humour and there are no really happy endings. In the few surviving portraits she appears haughty and forbidding, yet she seems to have made genuine friendships with Alastor the palmist and with Elisabetta, the little Italian girl who played the accordion in the streets of Norwich.

We know only what she wanted us to know, what she told journalists and interviewers, the stories she shared with friends. That carefully crafted image did not include any mention of the rift with her family; indeed, for the most part it did not include her family at all. Only in her later years, with both her parents safely dead, did she allude to the support they had given her and the people to whom they had introduced her, 'the best influences of the time in Norwich'. She was also loath to give credit to her teachers or to acknowledge the artists who had inspired her. Kate Nichols remains an enigma — but the following time line gives us some fixed points on which we have been able to hang our biography of her.

Timeline

1847 Oct. 5th	Born
1857 Spring	Birth of her brother Frederick Peter Nichols
c.1858–c.1865	(i.e. ages 11 to 18) At Mrs Dunnett's school. A sketchbook of 1859 survives.
1860	Birth of her brother and sister, the twins, Alfred Peter and Alice Emilia Sarah. Death of her grandmother, Sarah Nichols. Alpington Hall ceases to be the family home.
1865	'Coming out' party.
1866	Her father's mayoral year ran from November 1865 to November 1866. Kate attended numerous social events and made a presentation to the Princess of Wales when she visited Norwich with her husband and mother on 31st October 1866.
c.1868–73	At some point in this period Kate visits David Hall McKewan in London.
1870/71	Death of both her maternal grandparents. The family connection with Alton is severed.
1874/75	Spends two terms at the Norwich School of Art.
1875	First known dated etching — 'College' in Norwich Castle Museum.
1876/77/78	Visits France — Normandy and Barbizon.

1877	Exhibits at RA: 'Rue des Cordonniers, Dives, Normandy'. Dry-point.
1878	Exhibits at RA: 'Falling leaves, Barbizon, Forest of Fontainebleau'. Dry-point.
1878 Dec.	William Peter Nichols dies. Kate inherits £1,000.
1879–80	In Cornwall. Etching of Cornish scene in British Museum dated 1879. Etching of 'Pilchard boats at Newlyn' exhibited in Cornwall in 1880.
1879	Exhibits at RA:
	1. 'Ber St, Norwich' Dry-point.
	2. 'The thicket' Dry-point.
	3. 'Unlading' Dry-point.
1880	Royal Society of Painter-Etchers founded.
1881	At time of census Kate was in London in a lodging house — probably for the Painter-Etchers' 'all comers' exhibition which took place in the spring.
1881	Her sister, Alice, marries Reverend Arthur Wentworth Powell, former curate of St Stephen's in Norwich, and moves to Wales.
1882	Kate submitted two 'diploma works' to the RSPE, both dated 1881 — 'Fir trees' and 'Crown Point'. She was accepted on the first one and was made a Fellow.
1882	Exhibits at RA:
	1. 'A Norfolk Broad'
	2. 'Street in an old coaching town' Dry-point.
1882 Nov. 21st	Baptised into the Catholic Church.
1883	Exhibits at RA:
	1. 'Old houses, Norwich'
	2. 'Cow Hill, Norwich' Dry-point.
1884	'Old Biddy' — dated pencil sketch of a 100 year old lady in Norwich Castle Museum. One of a very few examples of Kate's figure drawing.
c.1884/85	Visits Lourdes and the High Pyrenees
1885	Norwich Art Circle founded. Swingeing criticism of her work in *Eastern Daily Press* in September.
1885	*A Few Words about the Catholic Church* published.
1886	*Novel of Old Norwich* published.
1887	*Two Norfolk Idylls* and *Musings at Cromer* published.
1888	Exhibits at the RA: 'Riverside, Norwich'.
1889	Foundation of Woodpecker Art Club. CMN made president.

5. 'Cow Hill', dry-point by Catherine Maude Nichols, exhibited at the Royal Academy in 1883. *Reproduced by kind permission of the British Museum.*

1889	Exhibits at the RA: 'Evening on the Broads'.
1889	Interview with the *Women's Penny Paper*.
1891	Exhibits at the RA: 'Strangers' Hall, Norwich'.
1890/91	Strangers' Hall pictures used as Christmas cards.
1892	*Zoroaster* and *Lines of Thought* published

1892 April/May	Exhibition 'Gleanings by Woodland and Wave' first in London (heavily advertised) and then in Royal Arcade, Norwich. It contained 150 works in various media.
1893	Two of her poems, 'Instead' and 'In Fairyland', published as songs, with music by Claud H. Hill, a Norwich schoolmaster. (A third poem, 'The dance of the leaves', would be published in the same way in 1897.)
1893	Elliot portrait of CMN painted.
1893	Very critical notice in the *Glasgow Herald*.
1893 Christmas	'Tsi-te-see, an Oriental fantasy' (story) published in *Atalanta* magazine. It was illustrated by M. Blake.
1894	Her sister, Alice Powell, dies.
1896	Her brother-in-law, Arthur Wentworth Powell, remarries. He also seems to have converted to Catholicism at this point and gone abroad, taking her niece and nephew with him.
1899/1900	Paints portrait of Elisabetta Capaldi.
c.1900	Moves to 73 Carlton Terrace.
1902	Kate's brother Frederick and his family living in Norwich — their youngest child, Philip Peter Ross Nichols, was born that year. Frederick's daughter, Margery, recalled living in Norwich 'for a time' and getting to know her grandmother. She did not mention her Aunt Kate.
1903	Article about CMN in *The Studio*.
1904	Matilda Nichols dies. Kate would have come into more of her father's money at this point. It also looks as if her brother Alfred moved in with her — he was certainly living with her in 1911.
1907	Exhibits at the Paris Salon. Article in *The Studio*. Publishes two dry-point etchings 'after Crome'.
1908	A busy year exhibition-wise. The *Norfolk Chronicle* reported in May that she was to exhibit a work at the Paris Salon, one at the RA and three miniatures at the Royal Institution and that she had been invited to submit work to the forthcoming Franco-British exhibition at Shepherds Bush. The work she submitted there was 'Old inn at Lakenham'.
1908–c.1910 (or later)	Involved with Alastor the Palmist.
1909	Made president of the Norwich branch of the National Anti-Vivisection Society.
1909	She was a signatory to a petition about acquiring, decorating

	and maintaining a Fine Art Pavilion for British Art at the Venice International Exhibition of Fine Arts.
1911	Visits Jersey and Germany — dated sketches in the Ashmolean.
1912	Her brother Frederick and his family move to the West Country. It is not clear where they had been before though we know they spent a good deal of time in India. Kate's exhibits at the Norwich Art Circle exhibition that year suggest she had recently visited Bristol so perhaps that is where they were living.
1913	The exhibits at the Norwich Art Circle exhibition this year suggest a recent visit to Cornwall.
1913	George Borrow 'centenary'. (He was actually born in 1803 so the celebrations were 10 years late!). Contributed etchings to the centenary booklet and produced a folder of four etchings for sale. Copied his portrait.
1913	Interview for *The Bookman*.
1916	Her nephew, Albon Wentworth Powell, killed in WWI. CMN seems not to have known.
1919	Last exhibit with Royal Society of Painter-Etchers
1921 Oct.	Exhibited at the Forum Club in Norwich. A work called 'Early spring, Norfolk' was singled out for special mention in the *Norfolk Chronicle*.
1921	Frederick Duleep Singh lectures to the Woodpecker Club at the Maddermarket Theatre. CMN's notes on the lecture survive. Lilly Bull says it was her last public appearance but —
1922	date of an oil painting of 'Open country, Hautbois' (came up for sale through Keys Fine Art Auction House on 12th April 2002). Hautbois is in Norfolk and some of her Banister relatives lived there.
1923 Jan.	Dies of cancer.

In the following chapters we shall do our best to illuminate as much of Kate's life and career as we can but much of it still remains as hidden as she wanted it to be. We have tried to delve beneath the persona she created for herself to see the real Catherine Maude Nichols, complicated and contradictory, generous and stern, devout and gullible, charming and forbidding, proud and self-deprecating, talented but unwilling to learn from others — but ultimately lonely and dissatisfied.

3

The Nichols family

Catherine Maude Nichols — Kate to her family and friends — was born into a large and prosperous middle-class family. For several generations the Nichols and the Musketts (her paternal grandmother's family) had been farmers and landowners in the parish of Alpington-with-Yelverton, two villages a few miles south-east of Norwich. William Peter Nichols, Catherine's father, and his brother and sisters had been born and brought up at Alpington Hall, a fine seventeenth-century red brick farm house with Dutch gables, now a listed building.

6. Alpington Hall, home of the Nichols family until 1860.
Kate would have visited her grandmother and aunts here.

Kate's paternal grandfather, Peter Nichols, died a few years before she was born, but she would have visited Alpington Hall to see her grandmother, Sarah, and her two unmarried aunts, Hannah and Eliza, who ran the farm with the help of a bailiff until old Mrs Nichols died in 1860. Kate's father's other two sisters, her Aunts Lucy and Sarah, both married. Sarah's husband was a captain in the Indian army and they lived abroad; Lucy was the wife of John Kerrison of Ranworth Hall and she had two sons who were some years older than Kate.

William Peter Nichols and his younger brother, James, were sent to the King Edward VI School (or Norwich Grammar School, now Norwich School) in the Cathedral Close in Norwich. It was one of the oldest schools in England, founded in 1096, and it provided the best education Norwich could offer at the time. William and James' headmaster was Reverend Edward Valpy (there from 1811 to 1829) who had a profound influence on the school's development. Within two years of his arrival he had increased the number of pupils from an all-time low of eight in 1811 to around three hundred. He was also notorious as a brutal disciplinarian, remembered by former pupils for his floggings, and by others for encouraging his pupils to be overly class conscious. His students later formed a society, the 'Valpeians', to which the Nichols brothers both belonged.[1] They probably joined the school some time between 1812 and 1815. Both the Nichols boys must have done well: they both opted to become surgeons and went to London to study — a somewhat unusual choice of career for young men from their background with a farm to inherit. In the eighteenth century surgeons had been called 'sawbones', often likened to butchers, and the job was seen as a trade rather than a profession — not a suitable calling for the sons of gentlemen. However, in the early years of the nineteenth century young men wanting to be surgeons first trained as physicians and attitudes to them were beginning to change.

James Nichols stayed in London and established a fashionable practice on Savile Row; he married a lady called Maria Pawley and they had nine children, the eldest of whom, Kate's cousin, William Pawley Nichols, became a talented engraver.[2] There was obviously an artistic streak in the Nichols family. William Peter Nichols returned to Norwich in the 1820s to set up his own practice.

Surgery in the 1820s was a risky business. Operations were carried out without anaesthetic, mostly in the patient's own home, and success was limited. Dr Nichols' patients (the practice of calling surgeons 'Mr' rather than 'Dr' was not universally observed in the early nineteenth century) paid for his services, but most chose to avoid his ministrations for as long as possible, calling him in only if their condition was life-threatening or had become unbearable. Even then, most of his work would have been relatively minor — lancing boils, letting blood, trussing hernias, dressing wounds and setting broken limbs. Surgeons performed invasive operations — like amputations — only in extreme cases because of the risk of post-operative infection. They operated in their street clothes and there was little understanding of the need for scrupulous cleanliness or the possibility of cross-infection. Surgeons like William Nichols who did post-mortems often brought infection to their living patients from the corpses on which they had been working. But techniques improved throughout his career. Dr Nichols would have seen the beginnings of anaesthesia, first with ether, then with chloroform, and the beginnings of antiseptics with the use of carbolic sprays.[3] The nineteeenth century was an exciting time to be a surgeon.

Not until 1850 did Dr Nichols secure one of the four coveted posts of surgeon to the Norfolk and Norwich Hospital[4] — posts coveted not for the salaries they offered, but because they gave the surgeons a supply of scalpel fodder, both living and dead, on which to practise their skills. It appears that he was a talented man, acknowledged by his peers to be exceptionally good at one of the nineteenth century's more reliable and dramatic operations — lithotomy. Lithotomy is the removal of stones from the bladder, kidney and gall bladder, but in the nineteenth century it applied almost exclusively to the removal of bladder stones. As late as 1936 Sir D'Arcy Power[5] described lateral lithotomy (the technique used for 75% of the Norwich operations) as 'the show test of a successful surgeon . . . the end was glorious, a surgical feat almost amounting to legerdemain, as, with a flourish, the surgeon removed the offending stone, which could be the size of a tennis ball, from the unfortunate patient's bladder.'

Norfolk had a particularly high incidence of bladder stones; various explanations have been put forward from the hard water which contains a large proportion of calcium to the poor diet of Norfolk labourers who subsisted largely

7. The Norfolk and Norwich Hospital c.1860. Kate Nichols' father was surgeon there from 1850.

on cereals with minimal amounts of milk and meat. Whatever the reasons, the condition was well documented from the seventeenth century onwards, but by the early twentieth century it had virtually disappeared. The Norwich and Norfolk Hospital had a series of talented surgeons who specialised in the operation and from the time the hospital opened in 1772 to 1909 they kept careful records of the numbers of lithotomies performed and made a comprehensive collection of the 1,408 stones they removed. In Norwich in 1779, one in every 55 admissions to the hospital was for bladder stone — as against one in every 1,650 admissions to the hospital in Cambridge, 1 in every 557 admissions to the Manchester Infirmary and one in every 287 in Newcastle-under-Lyme. Bladder stones cause agonising pain, and no doubt the presence of surgeons with a relatively successful track record in removing them contributed to the high level of admissions in Norwich at least as much as did the prevalence of the condition in the locality. In the early 1800s the mortality rate for this operation was roughly 1 in 7.[6]

Norwich soon became the place where surgeons came to learn to do lithotomies. William Peter Nichols was not one of the greatest exponents of the technique — that honour goes to men like William Cadge, William Donne, Philip Meadows Martineau, Edward Rigby, William Dalrymple and Dr Nichols' immediate predecessor as surgeon to the hospital, John Green Crosse — but nonetheless between 1850 and 1872 he performed the operation 75 times at the hospital and probably also on some of the patients in his private practice.[7] Another talented surgeon in Norwich who was Dr Nichols' contemporary was Edward Lubbock (1805–47), who was reputed to earn in the region of £4,000 a year.[8] Kate Nichols told The Bookman in 1913 that her father had been in partnership with Lubbock but there seems to be no evidence for this, though doubtless the two men knew each other and may even have been friends.

However, William Peter Nichols was an entrepreneur as well as a surgeon, and early in his career he lighted upon a lucrative and relatively simple way of capitalising on his medical training. He specialised in mental health — and in this his family background was very much to his advantage. Nineteenth century society was extremely class conscious and being treated by a gentleman, one whose family had been known to yours for generations, was highly desirable. And Dr Nichols often relied on his knowledge of Norfolk society. At the time of the infamous Windham lunacy case (see pages 32–33) part of the doctor's testimony about young Mr Windham related to having met him at a ball they had both attended. When the bankrupt and disgraced banker Sir Robert Harvey lay dying after an inept attempt to shoot himself, he allegedly invited William Peter Nichols to join him in a 'bottle of cool claret when I get over this', and after Sir Robert's death, Dr Nichols was able to assert that Sir Robert's problems with what he euphemistically described as 'excitement' were hereditary. 'I know that he inherits, or did inherit, a strong tendency to mental disorder,' Dr Nichols pronounced in court. 'He himself has always been, during my knowledge of him, very excitable, and on any sudden trouble that excitement becomes greater. I know that lately Sir Robert had been subject to great excitement from several causes. I had seen him professionally respecting such excitement.'[9] Of course, by implying that Sir Robert had killed himself while the balance of his mind was disturbed, William Nichols ensured that the Harveys could give Sir Robert a proper burial, rather than the hole-and-corner, after-dark ritual that he would have had as a suicide were he deemed to have been sane.

As well as his private practice, Dr Nichols also opened a lunatic asylum for gentlefolk. It was not the first such institution in Norwich; the Heigham Retreat had been founded in 1829 by Dr Jollye of Loddon. The Retreat was a genteel establishment, taking around fifteen patients who were cared for by a staff of eight or nine 'attendants' as nurses in lunatic asylums were then called, and five chambermaids. This was an exceptionally high staff/patient ratio — in the public asylums the ratio of patients to attendants was more like twenty to one. For a few years Mr Jollye took Dr Nichols on as a partner, but in 1836 William Peter Nichols opened his own asylum at Heigham House, just down the road from Heigham Retreat.

He took into partnership a young doctor called John Ferra Watson. Dr Watson had broken his leg as a boy and it had been so inexpertly set that it continued to trouble him all his adult life and made him unable to cope with working as a

8. *Heigham Hall Asylum, run by Kate's father, William Peter Nichols, and Dr John Ferra Watson.*

general practitioner which had been his original choice of career. But Heigham House was just the start. Over the next few years William Nichols spent a good deal of time and effort mortgaging his family's property in and around Norwich to buy a larger house, Heigham Hall, which he knew was coming on the market. No doubt his choice of location was dictated by the availability of suitable properties, but it does seem rather unprofessional to have opened a rival asylum so close to the Retreat — Heigham Hall was almost directly opposite — and it shows Dr Nichols' ruthless streak. He and Dr Watson opened their new establishment in 1841,[10] and at the time of the census it had a similar number of patients to Heigham Retreat — but they employed fewer staff, presumably to keep costs low. By 1859 they had put the Retreat out of business. They bought the building, transferred the patients to their own establishment and sold Heigham Retreat and the surrounding land for building. Within two years they had nearly sixty patients and a staff/patient ratio of one to six. However, they still offered a level of care for which the well-to-do were willing to pay.

Although the Norfolk County Lunatic Asylum had been established in 1812, it had a fearsome reputation and wealthy families were unwilling to entrust their relatives to its care, even as paying patients. A private asylum, run by gentlemen, in a grand house with spacious grounds, was infinitely preferable. The census returns (except for the 1841 ones) mask Dr Nichols' patients behind initials, but they do tell us what they had done for a living in the outside world. There were clergymen and doctors, solicitors and merchants and numerous 'gentlemen' and 'gentlewomen'. They suffered, no doubt, from conditions we would today label as stress, nervous breakdown, depression, panic attacks and personality disorders, and more serious ones like psychosis or brain damage brought about by accidents or repeated, uncontrolled epileptic fits. Many female patients suffered from what we now recognise as post-natal depression. These were the conditions the public asylums treated and recorded, and there is no reason to suppose that patients in private asylums were very different.

Dr Watson became superintendent of the asylum, his wife supervised the women's part of the establishment, and they and their four children lived in some style in one wing of the house. It was a relatively easy job in that the asylum was only licensed to take sixty-five patients and their day-to-day care was in the hands of the nursing staff. Dr Watson would have attended to the physical ailments of his charges, but there were no treatments for most of the psychological conditions he was dealing with. Patients either got better with a period of rest and recuperation, or they remained in the asylum indefinitely, and the more unmanageable ones were prescribed sedatives or kept in secure conditions. Families were relieved to have their more embarrassing members cared for out of sight and out of mind, and they were willing to pay handsomely for the privilege — there are indications that the fees could be as much as £100 a year, an astronomical sum in the mid-nineteenth century. Many of Heigham Hall's patients were there for many years, and the 'hatched, matched and despatched' columns of the local newspapers recorded the deaths — by name — of inmates who were elderly and had been at Heigham for many years. A few committed suicide, one or two escaped, some were kept 'under restraint' in straitjackets or locked rooms, but most accounts of Heigham Hall suggest it was well run and reasonably comfortable. William Peter Nichols visited the asylum from time to time, but essentially he was a sleeping partner, making money from his investment but doing very little of the work.

He was very successful but his judgement was not always good. In or around 1844, for example, when he was staying at Felbrigg — another indication of his position in county society — Dr Nichols was called upon to examine little William Frederick Windham, then aged about four. The little boy was obviously rather backward, dribbled a lot and couldn't talk properly, and he paid no attention to his toys or to the watch which was dangled before him. Dr Nichols did not mince his words. He informed the boy's father bluntly that the child was an imbecile. He could not know the use to which this information would be put many years later, but it was a brutal, tactless — and ultimately inaccurate — judgement. He was never invited to Felbrigg again.

The dribbling and the speech impediment were attributable to the boy's hare lip. William Frederick Windham's parents were themselves unstable and alternately spoilt and abused him so that he grew up insecure, violent, unruly and lacking self-control. He was not particularly bright, but, though he was eventually expelled, he went to Eton where he earned the unfortunate soubriquet 'Mad Windham'. He later commanded a troop of yeomanry. His behaviour as a young man was loutish and eccentric in the extreme, he was far happier with working men than he was with people of his own class (and they tolerated him because he was generous with his money), he was mad about railway engines — and he made an extremely foolish marriage to a 'pretty horse breaker' (one of the young ladies of dubious virtue who rode up and down Rotten Row) and she almost ruined him — but he was by no means the only young aristocrat to behave so badly. Unfortunately for him, his father died before he reached his majority and he was put in the care of his uncle, Colonel Windham, who wanted the Felbrigg estate for himself. The colonel therefore tried to have his nephew declared insane. The trial was a hugely expensive and unedifying cause célèbre in the winter of 1861–62; 200 witnesses were called of whom Dr William Peter Nichols was one. Many of them were discredited — it was obvious that Colonel Windham had paid them to exaggerate his nephew's failings — but William Nichols' original diagnosis of imbecility could not be ignored. However, in the end the case failed and young Mr Windham was declared to be sane enough to look after his own affairs.[11]

In 1846, at the comparatively late age of 45, William Peter Nichols felt he was sufficiently established to take a wife. The lady he chose was Matilda Mary Banister, daughter of John Banister, the Rector of Kelvedon Hatch in Essex and Perpetual Curate of West Worldham in Hampshire. John Banister came from Kent and was the son of a gentry family, a younger son who had to make his own way in the world. He had been at West Worldham since 1818 and Matilda was born there. She was the only girl in a house full of young men, for not only did she have four brothers, her father supplemented the £80 a year his curacy paid by running a school for teenage boys. He was not appointed to the living at Kelvedon Hatch until 1841, and though Matilda was married in her father's church there, the family do not really seem to have spent much time in Essex — her father took his salary

9. *Rev. John Banister, Kate Nichols' maternal grandfather. The label on the back of the photograph suggests that it once belonged to the Nichols family — it lists Matilda Nichols' (née Banister) children but not those of her brothers.*
Reproduced by kind permission of Personalia.

and then paid part of it to a curate to run the parish for him while the Banisters continued to live in Hampshire. To begin with, that curate was Matilda's eldest brother, William, but within a matter of months William Banister became Vicar of High Laver, just down the road from Kelvedon, and the curacy, and tenancy of the Rectory, passed to Reverend Frederick Fane, a member of a local land-owning family. Such arrangements were quite common in the nineteenth century when many parish clergy were poorly paid and men needed several salaries to be able to support their families in a manner befitting their status.

Matilda's mother was born Mary Matilda Shuttleworth, to an English family living in Denmark, but beyond that we know very little about her. Confusingly for the genealogist, the Banisters christened their only daughter Matilda Mary, and even more confusingly, she was often called 'Maude', even in official documents like her husband's will.

Matilda Mary Banister was 26 when she married William Peter Nichols, some 19 years his junior. Catherine Maude — Kate — was the couple's first child, born just 14 months after the wedding, on 5th October 1847. Dr Nichols had bought a fine house in Surrey Street, number 32, as a home for his family. Contemporary accounts describe it as a three-storey Georgian property, and though it no longer exists it was probably very similar to the houses still standing on the opposite side of the street — numbers 29 to 35. The family lived in considerable comfort with a live-in cook and housemaid, a nursemaid for little Catherine, and a resident groom who would be on hand to drive the carriage at any time of day or night if Dr Nichols was called out to an emergency.

10. The surviving Georgian houses on Surrey Street. The Nichols' home was opposite and probably fairly similar to one of these houses.

We do not know a great deal about Kate's Banister relatives. Her uncle William Banister was a clergyman who spent much of his career in Liverpool, but of her uncles Frederick and John we can find no trace. However, in 1857, Kate's fourth uncle, Edward Banister, was appointed Vicar of Besthorpe, probably through the good offices of his sister and brother-in-law. Besthorpe is near Attleborough and lies some fifteen miles south-west of Norwich. Edward Banister and his wife, Eliza Ann, had seven children, and one of the older girls, Constance Mary, became a lifelong friend of Kate's.

11. 'The Bethel Hospital', dry-point by Catherine Maude Nichols.
Her father was surgeon to the hospital and her younger brother played the organ there.
She also made an oil painting of the same scene.

In 1850 Dr Nichols was at last appointed surgeon to the hospital and no doubt his workload increased. He had also been appointed surgeon to the Bethel Hospital, police surgeon and surgeon to the prison — jobs that attracted prestige, an honorarium and regular appearances in the press. It was Dr Nichols, for example, who was called in when the notorious James Rush shot Isaac Jermy; it was Dr Nichols who misidentified some of the pieces of flesh and bone (because they had been soaked in hot water and looked like the body parts of a young woman) belonging to the unfortunate Martha Sheward whose husband murdered her and then distributed bits of her body around the city; it was Dr Nichols who cheerfully pronounced Sarah Hannah Barker insane when she was aggressive and abusive after being caught with a wad of counterfeit banknotes.[12] One wonders how much Matilda and Kate, cocooned in the comfort of 32 Surrey Street, really knew of the seamier side of the career of their husband and father.

Dr Nichols was an ambitious man and his ambition extended well beyond his profession. In 1837 when the Act requiring that births, marriages and deaths be reported to a civilian registrar came into force, Dr Nichols had got himself appointed registrar for the Mancroft district. He was also becoming involved in local politics as a member of the City Council; in time he would become a member of the Watch Committee and the Gaol Committee, and in the 1860s he would chair the Cattle Plague Committee, set up to deal with the spread of a particularly contagious form of viral disease that attacked, and usually killed, cattle.[13] By 1853 he had become a magistrate, sitting on the Bench almost every week. In 1870 he would play a major part in national politics, supporting Mr

12. The Royal visitors in St Andrew's Hall 1866. This was where 18 year old Kate presented an album to the Princess of Wales.

Tillett, Liberal candidate for Norwich.[14] But the pinnacle of Dr Nichols' civic career came in November 1865 when he took his turn as Lord Mayor of Norwich. He presided at various grand gatherings and, honour of honours, entertained the Prince and Princess of Wales when they visited Norwich with the Queen of Denmark on Wednesday 31st October 1866. Matilda and Kate were present at the Guildhall that day to hear the speeches; they then followed the royal party to St Andrew's Hall where 19-year-old Kate presented an album of photographs to the Princess on behalf of the ladies of Norwich. It was a splendid object with a silver-gilt cover, lined in blue watered silk, and bearing the Princess's monogram, Prince of Wales feathers and the crest of the City of Norwich. Inside were photos of Norwich buildings and civic dignitaries in hand-painted frames. Dr Nichols and Matilda attended the banquet at Costessey for the royal visitors and Kate joined them for the ball that followed.[15]

However, all William Peter Nichols' hopes and ambitions had nearly been derailed in the early 1850s by his involvement in a particularly unsavoury episode. In June 1852, Reverend Edmund Holmes, curate of Hethersett, was accused of the rape of a little girl, Sarah Ann Bunn. Her mother had returned home from church to find the curate and her daughter on the bed together. She called the constable and Holmes was, quite reasonably, taken into custody, but in view of his status as 'a member of a high County family', the magistrate withheld the arrest warrant and contacted George Holmes, Edmund's brother, who just happened to be a magistrate. Even the law was class conscious in the nineteenth century – the magistrate's clerk later admitted that a poor man would have been treated very differently.

George Holmes was actually Edmund's half-brother, and both he and William Waite Andrews, the Vicar of Hethersett (and technically Edmund's employer), were desperate to hush up the scandal. They contacted Dr Nichols to ask him to take Edmund into his asylum. In those days there was no psychological assessment of criminals – without intervention from friends and family Holmes would have faced transportation for life; rape is a serious crime and up to 1841 it had attracted the death penalty. It may be that Edmund Holmes was indeed mentally ill, and the fact that he had spoken of his intentions towards the girl earlier in the day to his housekeeper – who was the child's aunt – does suggest that perhaps he was not in his right mind. She and her husband both gave evidence to the effect that Reverend George Holmes was prone to violent attacks of temper and they had on occasion had to restrain him physically. It later transpired that some two years earlier George Holmes had asked Dr Nichols to assess his brother, but at that point William Nichols had not felt Edmund was ill enough to require treatment.

Even in 1852 it was not possible to place someone in a lunatic asylum without due process. Heigham Hall was licensed, and though patients could admit themselves voluntarily, a person who was already in custody needed to be certified and the certification had to be signed by two doctors other than the owners of the asylum. William Peter Nichols did what he had probably done in previous cases and approached two of his hospital colleagues; one, Dr Taylor, agreed to sign but the other, Dr Hull, refused on the grounds that the certification was purely to help a rapist evade justice. Dr Nichols then approached Dr Gillett, the medical officer in Loddon, and he provided the necessary signature. George Holmes signed as magistrate. William Peter Nichols then presented the certificate to the constable and Edmund Holmes was duly released into his care.

Thus far Dr Nichols' actions could be construed as reasonable, even though Dr Hull would not have agreed. It may be that the two men had had previous disagreements, it may be that Dr Hull had a particular aversion to men who assaulted little girls, it may be that he resented the amount of money Messrs Nichols and Watson were making from their asylum — in future testimony he would claim that Dr Nichols had said Edmund Holmes' admission was 'worth £100 a year in his pocket'.

In June 1854 matters came to a head — the two-year delay is curious but probably came about because Dr Hull knew that that was when the licence for Heigham Hall was due for renewal. There was a most unseemly exchange between the two men, in public, and the matter was brought before the magistrates. This was doubly embarrassing because both men were themselves on the Bench, and the magistrate's discomfiture in sentencing his fellows is palpable even in the newspaper reports. He tried several times to persuade the two doctors to apologise to each other, even suggesting the form of words they could use, but both were adamant that they were not at fault. In the end they were both bound over to keep the peace.

That same month, William Peter Nichols and John Ferra Watson were called upon to account for their behaviour before the Committee of Visitors, the governing body of their asylum. Witnesses were called, and the case of Edmund Holmes and the little girl from Hethersett was described in some detail. The Visitors were forced to acknowledge that the paperwork was in order; Edmund Holmes' admission to Heigham Hall was in accordance with the law, even if they privately suspected that the signatures of the certifying doctors had been given without their ever having examined the patient. But not content with admitting Edmund Holmes to the asylum, if Dr Hull is to be believed, William Peter Nichols had openly boasted about how he had rescued a member of his own class from the 'gripe of the law'. He also made another extremely unwise decision. In September 1852 he appointed Holmes chaplain to Heigham Hall Asylum! The Visitors demanded an explanation. Dr Watson pointed out loyally that the clergyman had carried out his duties 'assiduously' and that he had recently accepted the post of curate under Reverend J. W. Cobb at St Margaret's, Norwich, but the Visitors were unimpressed. They reprimanded Dr Nichols and Dr Watson for appointing a former patient to the post of chaplain and only agreed to renew their licence because a third doctor, William Harcourt Ranking, a man they believed to be of irreproachable character, was to become a partner at Heigham Hall. Only if Dr Ranking agreed to take an active role in the running of the asylum could Heigham Hall continue in business.[16]

It was an unpleasant affair and it had many repercussions. Questions were asked in Parliament and the case was examined in *The Lancet*. Letters appeared in the national press. The conclusion was that Holmes had indeed been mentally ill, his admission to Heigham Hall had been appropriate – and Dr Hull was branded a bitter and vindictive man. Furthermore, it was later alleged, there had been no rape, no attempted rape – just a minor sexual assault. Whether Sarah Ann and her family would have agreed is open to question. It is still difficult to be sure who was in the right, but the appointment of Holmes does seem to have been a particularly curious one, as does Dr Nichols' assertion that after just 12 weeks Edmund Holmes was cured and perfectly fit to resume his profession. There were some questions about why he had been allowed to continue to live at the asylum after the Visitors insisted he be forced to resign the post of chaplain – but in the end, Heigham Hall and its proprietors were exonerated. However, in December 1854 the Church of England finally intervened. The Bishop of Norwich approached the Rector of St Margaret's and asked him to dismiss Edmund Holmes from his post of curate. Thereafter, Edmund Holmes retired home to Brooke Hall, and though he was not formally unfrocked he never practised his profession again.[17]

Such episodes are interesting in that they help us build a picture of William Peter Nichols – which is important because we know so very little of the people who shaped Kate Nichols' character. Of her mother we know nothing beyond her name – we do not even have family photographs from which we could draw the most simplistic of conclusions about her personality. Though Kate had nephews and nieces none of them seem to have had children, and the immediate family line died out with Kate's youngest nephew, Philip Ross Nichols, in 1975. At that point, if not before, family photographs would probably have been disposed of or destroyed, so we have no idea what Kate looked like as a young girl and even less idea about her mother and siblings.

For all his importance and influence in Norwich it was even difficult to find an image of William Peter Nichols. He was a very ambitious man, ruthless when it suited him, and not particularly concerned with what others thought — characteristics which Kate seems to have inherited. His judgement was not always sound and he was excessively proud of his social position. He obviously imbued his eldest daughter with a strong sense of her family's social status — she made much of it in the many interviews she gave. We can also deduce that the good doctor had a slightly eccentric sense of humour, demonstrated in his description of his family for the census enumerator in 1871. Catherine and her cousin Constance are listed as 'English maidens' — a courteously old fashioned description which probably displeased Kate who already considered herself to be a professional artist. His wife he described as 'Jack of All Trades' implying, one hopes, that she did everything in the household, rather than that she was 'Master of None' as the complete saying goes.

In an interview in 1913 Kate claimed that William Nichols was her great champion and that he encouraged and nurtured her artistic career. We know very little about Kate's early life but it seems more than likely that her father was too busy to pay much attention to her and that she actually spent a good deal of her early childhood with her mother and other adults. The surviving 1859 sketchbook[18] is inscribed 'Catherine Maude Nichols from Mama June 1859 Surry [sic] Street'. Many of the pictures in it are of Alton — perhaps she was given it to use during her summer holiday. (See plates 18a and b.)

The writing appears to be Catherine's, though it is much neater and smaller than her adult hand, and the inscription continues rather oddly 'Mama is coming to Alton today. Oh! Oh! Oh!' It is hard to know how to interpret this — was she happy to be seeing her mother again? Apprehensive about what her mother would think of her holiday sketches? Excited to be going home? Sorry the holiday was nearly over? We have no way of knowing.

In the spring of 1857, when Kate was nine, Matilda Nichols gave birth to her second child, a little boy they named Frederick Peter. Three years later came the twins, Alice and Alfred, born when their mother was forty. Quite why the Nichols left such a long gap between their first and second children we do not know, but what is certain is that by the age of thirteen Kate was no longer the sole focus of her parents' attention. We do not know whether she resented the younger children, whether they aroused her maternal instincts or whether she was completely uninterested in what went on in the nursery of 32 Surrey Street under the jurisdiction of Nanny Adcock and Nurse Watson. Certainly she does not seem to have been close to her siblings — in fact, in all her numerous interviews she never once mentions their existence.

In due course, Frederick Peter was sent to Shrewsbury School. He went on to Cambridge, trained at Barts, became an army surgeon and eventually rose to the

13. Kate's brother, Frederick Peter Nichols, in the Rugby team at Shrewsbury School, c.1872. He is seated in the front row, third from the right. Reproduced by kind permission of Shrewsbury School.

rank of Lieutenant Colonel. In the late 1880s he married Florence Ross, daughter of the Vicar of Alderney in the Channel Islands, and they had four children. They spent time in India before returning to live in the West Country when Frederick retired in 1912.[19]

The two youngest Nichols children seem to have been less robust and fared less well than their elder siblings – as might be expected of twins born in 1860 to a comparatively elderly mother who would have received very little in the way of antenatal care. It is possible that Alfred was delicate for, unlike his elder brother, he was not sent away to school. He never married and never seems to have had a proper job, though he was musical and was 'a familiar figure in many Norwich institutions' where he played the organ. He was very involved with the Church of England and no fewer than eight clergymen were present at his funeral, including the vicars of St James, All Saints-with-St Julian and St Barnabas, Norwich and St Mark's, Lakenham.[20] He lived at home until his mother's death in 1904 and then seems to have moved in with Kate. He spent the last two years of his life in lodgings at Hackford, possibly because he needed some form of nursing care.

Alice, his twin, married young, in 1881. Her husband, Arthur Wentworth

Powell, was Curate of St Stephen's, then at Hoveton, but soon after the marriage they moved to Wales where he had been appointed Chaplain and Private Secretary to the Bishop of St David's. It was a prestigious job but does not seem to have included a house — the family led a peripatetic existence moving from lodging house to lodging house. Alice had two children, Gwladys and Albon, but died in 1894 when they were still quite small. Two years later Arthur remarried and the family disappear from the records. We think they went abroad. However we do know that at about that point Arthur left the Church of England and became a Roman Catholic. By 1911 he was back in England, working as an insurance agent — and in 1912 he changed his mind again and was received back into the Church of England. He ended his days as Vicar of Minley in Hampshire — something of a sinecure as Minley was an army base and most services there were taken by the chaplain while Arthur continued to live in Hammersmith.[21]

Kate's relationship with her brothers and sister seems to have remained distant, and as far as we can tell she had little contact with her nephews and nieces. Alice's children are mentioned in her will — but she seems not to have known that by the time she wrote it Albon had been dead for seven years. He was an adventurous young man who joined the merchant navy and then took a job with the Buenos Aires and Pacific Railway in Argentina. The railway sent a contingent of young men to fight in the First World War; Albon was one of them and he was killed in 1916.[22]

Kate may have known Frederick's children slightly better for they did live in Norwich for a time and in October 1902 one of Kate's entries in the Norwich Art Circle exhibition was a miniature of her 12-year-old niece, 'Miss Marjery [sic] Nichols, daughter of Lieut. Col. F.P.Nichols RAMC.' Sadly, this picture seems to have disappeared, as have the ones we know she drew of her father.

Kate's youngest nephew, Philip Peter Ross Nichols, Margery's brother, was born in Norwich in 1902. He is better known as 'Ross Nichols' or 'Nuinn', an eccentric who was probably the member of the family most like his Aunt Kate. He was a teacher, but in the long holidays he wrote poetry, painted, and indulged his interest in naturism and is remembered as a significant figure in the Bardic movement. Numerous photographs survive of him, incongruously dressed in druid robes — he is one of the few members of Kate's family of whom we have pictures.[23]

Frederick's older children were apparently much more conventional. His eldest son, Francis, was a career soldier who was lost at sea in the Second World War, while his daughters led lives of quiet spinsterly respectability in the West Country. If Kate ever visited them, no record of the visits remains.

In the many interviews she gave to journalists Kate Nichols always implied

14. *Kate's nephew, Ross Nichols or 'Nuinn'.*
He was an important figure in the Bardic
movement. Reproduced by kind permission of
Philip Carr-Gomm.

that she was a single-minded spinster with no close relatives, someone who devoted herself entirely to her art. The reality was rather different. At the time of her death Kate had two brothers living, three nieces and two nephews and at least a dozen cousins, many of whom were married with children. Presumably she felt that being a member of a large family was at odds with the picture of a selfless, dedicated artist that she wanted to present to the world. It is not the only example of the way she bent the truth to enhance her image.

4

'No professors ever instructed me'

Kate Nichols was also economical with the truth when it came to describing her artistic education. 'I am self-taught,' she told *The Bookman* in 1913. 'No professors ever instructed me in the use of oils, watercolours or the etching tool, nor have I ever been taught miniature work of which I have done not a little.' She was always anxious to present herself this way — perhaps to deflect any criticism of the quality of her work. And criticisms there sometimes were — the Norwich papers were often quite rude about her pictures[1] and in March 1892, by which time Kate was in her forties and at the height of her artistic career, a critic in the *Glasgow Herald* wrote a rather unkind review of the annual exhibition of the Royal Society of Painter-Etchers and singled her work out for comment. 'It is ungracious to specify any one artist unfavourably when a solitary sinner or one in a small company,' he began, 'but as we can also add a good word for her occasional grace and fancy, we may say that Miss C. M. Nichols . . . would do well to practise drawing vigorously before trusting as much to the acid and the needle. There is, in a word, too much display of indifferent draughtsmanship at the present show.'[2] Kate must have been mortified.

****

We know nothing of her childhood but by the time she was in her teens Kate was a pupil at Mrs Dunnett's School. The school opened in 1858 on Surrey Street, a few yards away from Kate's home, and quickly acquired a reputation for excellence. Mrs Dunnett was the daughter of a Norwich-born gentleman and teacher, Christopher Thurgar, and the wife of a successful accountant. She had four children of her own and she also took a handful of girls as boarders, but most of her pupils seem to have been day girls who lived in the city, the daughters of well-to-do professionals and businessmen. The teaching concentrated on history, literature and modern languages.

Kate's friend Mary Mann wrote a novel called *Gran'ma's Jane* which was set in the Norwich of the 1860s. Most of Mary Mann's scenarios were based on real places or events; in this work, little Jane attends the annual children's ball at St Andrew's Hall and shows off the steps she had learnt at dancing class. 'Jane was made by her elders to place her silk shod feet in first, second and third positions before she left, she went through the polka, the waltz, the varsovienne steps, she held out her tarlatan skirts and courtesied [sic] to the floor.' In 1856, 9-year-old Kate Nichols attended the Mayor's Juvenile Ball at the Assembly Rooms along with two or three hundred other boys and girls from the wealthier Norwich families. The newspaper report makes it clear that this was a one-off event, an attempt by the then mayor to revive what had been a tradition earlier in the century. Many of the children wore fancy dress, but it looks as if Kate was not one of them.[3] Presumably she too had had dancing lessons and could waltz and curtsey and dance the polka and the varsovienne — and as late as 1912 when she submitted an entry to Cox's *Who's Who in Norfolk and Suffolk* (aged 65) she listed 'dancing' as one of her hobbies, along with reading and the theatre.

In the novel Jane is also sent to 'Mrs Bennett's Establishment for Young Ladies' which is actually Mrs Dunnett's school — 'Bennett'/'Dunnett', even the owners' names are similar. Mary Mann describes the white scrubbed floorboards in the schoolroom and the narrow benches and tables where the girls sat to work. They each had a bookshelf and their books were 'veiled in the green jaconet lining [a cheap fabric] with which all the school books were clothed.' She mentions in particular Brewer's *Guide to English History*, Delille's *French Grammar* and a particular favourite, Tasso's *Gerusalemme Liberata* — Mrs Dunnett herself seems to have specialised in teaching Italian and Kate and her friends learnt great swathes of Tasso by heart.

There were no organised games: 'No tennis in those days, or hockey, or cricket for schoolgirls. A game of Les Graces, perhaps, of battledore and shuttlecock for the more actively inclined'; 'Les Graces' involved whirling a beribboned hoop round in a circle towards your opponent who tried to catch it on a wand. The action was a bit like throwing a frisbee. It was pretty and graceful to watch and was thought especially suitable for young girls. In their breaks the girls who were not playing these sedate games 'sauntered about with their arms around each other's waists or sat reading under the trained branches of the willow tree.'[4] It all sounds very gentle and civilised.

15. Kate's friend, Polly Rackham (later
Mary E. Mann) c.1870.

Mrs Dunnett had her favourites, and an invitation survives from about 1870 in which she says 'I should so like to have with me at the same time three of the "olden time"' — and the three she had in mind were Polly Rackham (who became Mary Mann), Kate Nichols and Rachel Taylor, all of whom were by then in their early twenties.[5] The school had just moved from Surrey Street to new premises — Denbigh House on Newmarket Road — so perhaps Mrs Dunnett wanted to show the new building off to her former pupils. All three seem to have been clever, lively girls and in the school holidays, and for a few years after they left school, they wrote to each other frequently. In the 1860s respectable young girls could not come and go as they pleased — even meeting a friend to go for a walk had to be carefully organised and approved by one's parents, and of course any evening activity or out-of-town excursion required a chaperone. Letters were the only way the girls could keep in touch with each other, even though most of them lived within walking distance of each other's homes. Polly was a hoarder, and many of the notes she received survive.[6] The ones from Kate are fairly banal — cancelling an arrangement to meet at the library because her parents had made other plans, enquiring whether the girls were going to see each other at a local opera performance and, in one very apologetic letter explaining at length how she really had returned Polly's copy of a two-volume history book. 'You know Polly, I am so afraid of you that of course I can't write naturally,' she explained

16. Letter from Kate Nichols to Polly Mann, dated May 1866.

on page three of the missive. 'When I had written the first page I started in terror and blotted the whole thing.' All the friends seem to have been in awe of Polly Rackham who was clever, charismatic and always had a string of boyfriends in tow, but from what we know of Kate Nichols it seems likely that this was a tongue-in-cheek comment. These letters were written when she was in her late teens and they are much neater than the few later ones that survive with their sprawling handwriting and copious under-linings for emphasis.

Rachel Taylor's letters are full of slang, in-jokes and enthusiasm for life. One she wrote from Cromer ran 'I have bathed three times. Oh splendid! Beautiful! Glorious!' Rachel's father had been a solicitor but he died when she was quite young so her mother was in charge of the household. Mrs Taylor seems to have been strict — Rachel often had to write to cancel arrangements to meet in town or go for a walk, and in one letter she says she has, inexplicably, been forbidden to write to her friends except on Sundays. Rachel seems to have been particularly fond of Kate, indeed, if we did not know that young women in the nineteenth century were given to excesses of affection we might suspect that the two were rather more than friends. 'My best love to my chum Katie' wrote Rachel on one occasion, 'I miss her tre......ly'. The Taylors were staying in Cromer for three months on account of Mrs Taylor's poor health. Rachel had been taken out of school for the duration and had a governess whom she disliked. Kate had been invited to stay with them for a couple of weeks and the girls had obviously had fun — there was an incident with Rachel's governess's sister 'the other Rayner' and a bathing machine that Rachel urged Polly to ask Kate about. Rachel also told Polly, 'Of course I immensely enjoyed Katie's stay here,' and enquired, 'Do you think her brown?' Today that comment would suggest a healthy tan from exposure to the sea air, but in the 1870s a brown complexion was considered unattractive and unladylike. Kate is often described as 'sallow' — it may be that days outdoors at the seaside had darkened her skin to something she and Rachel considered ugly. In another letter Rachel comments on how well Kate looked after a visit to Alton to see her grandparents — 'I never saw such a deal of good as her Hampshire visit has done her. I never saw her so fat' — another comment that has a totally different meaning to a twenty-first-century reader. Kate was always thin and bony — 'fat' was a compliment implying she looked healthy and well fed.

Yet another of Rachel's comments after a different visit casts a completely new light on Kate's character. 'You never saw such a dissatisfied girl as Katie is,' she confided to Polly, 'she has two dances on hand and the Orpheus affair [a performance they were all going to] and she does nothing but grumble for more invitations.' At seventeen, Kate was apparently something of a party girl! Rachel

also hints that for a time at least Kate enjoyed a flirtation with a young man — 'Kate's friend, Dick' features in several letters and for a time Rachel only hears of Kate through him. 'I hear Kate is back in Norfolk,' she sniffed, 'through Dick Currie to whom alone she has found time to write.' The Taylors had connections in Hingham and Reverend M. W. Currie was the vicar there — it seems likely 'Dick' was related to the Vicarage family though we do not know for sure. However, in August 1864 Dick went off to Rome and that is the last we hear of him.

Another of Kate's friends was Isabel Mears and her parents were elderly and seem to have been quite controlling. Isabel and her sister were removed from the relatively liberal atmosphere of Mrs Dunnett's school and sent to board at a school run by a clergyman and his wife near Gainsborough in Lincolnshire —

Catherine Maude Nichols from The Women's Penny Paper, *July 1889. This is the earliest picture of her that we have.*

Kate visited her there and reported that she was lonely and unhappy. Isabel was depressive and in her many long, self-absorbed letters to Polly she complains that she has not heard from Kate — and on the one occasion when she does see her she is keen to tell Polly — quite inaccurately as it turned out — 'Kate Nichols is not, I believe, as strong as she used to be.' In Isabel Mears' world everyone was ill or unhappy or riding for a fall. 'I am so glad Mr Nichols is going to be mayor,' she wrote in November 1865, 'fancy the festival. Vanity — vanity - vanity — pleasure never comes when we expect her . . .' and there was a lot more in the same vein.

The girls all valued their education; their letters are full of descriptions of books they read and music they enjoyed, copies of poems and erudite observations. No doubt they were trying to impress each other. Kate, for example, claimed to have loved Byron's *Bride of Abydos*, regarded Walter Scott's *The Lord of the Isles* as greatly inferior to 'Lallah' (presumably Thomas Moore's *Lallah Rookh*) and enjoyed opera but often regarded the plots as 'stupid'. She was very impressed by a book Mrs Dunnett gave her called *The Gentle Life*. This was written by James Hain Friswell and was first published in 1864; it became enormously popular and ran to over 20 editions. It was a collection of essays with titles like 'On the Difference between leading the Gentle Life and being Genteel', 'Upon the Alleged Equality of Man', 'On what is called Etiquette', 'On Male and Female Flirts', 'Principally concerning Men's Wives' and a parallel chapter concerning 'Women's Husbands', 'Successful People' and 'Regarding the Company we Keep'. Kate thought it 'splendid . . . not at all stiff and so jolly' which seems a slightly odd description for a serious book by a devoutly Christian author.

Mrs Dunnett was obviously encouraging Kate and her other pupils to think, to learn modern languages, study history and appreciate literature. But attitudes to girls' education were still contradictory. In the mid-1860s when Kate and her friends left school there was still not a great deal they could do with their education. Not until 1869 did the first few women get the chance of a university education — Girton College, Cambridge opened that year, but even then the young women were housed at Hitchin, well away from the male undergraduates and the life of the university proper. Many people still genuinely believed that women's and men's brains were different, and fears were expressed in the press about the well-being of young girls taxing their intellects in such an apparently unnatural way.

Kate's family were liberal, their home was a meeting place for the intelligentsia and the influential of Norwich, their house was filled with pictures and they were happy to pay for their daughter to be educated — but at the end of the day they would still have expected her to marry; marriage was the only career open to respectable girls. Three of Kate's friends, Nellie Edgar, Julie Woolbright and Polly

Rackham, did what was expected of them and married young; Isabel Mears took the only career option open to her and became a governess; poor Rachel, the liveliest of Mrs Dunnett's three favourites, was kept at home with her domineering mother and sister and gradually she stopped writing to her former school fellows. Meanwhile, the Nichols did their best to help Kate find a husband. In one letter to Polly Rackham, Rachel Taylor comments on the splendid 'coming-out' party that Kate had had. This probably took place in 1865. Kate was eighteen that October and by then the family would have known that her father was likely to be elected mayor the following month. Inevitably he would host and attend dinners and balls, luncheon parties and soirées, lectures and concerts — ideal opportunities for his daughter to meet eligible young men. We know from press reports that Kate did indeed attend a number of civic events in 1865–66 and no doubt there were others that went unreported.

No pictures survive of her as a young girl, but the portrait of her painted in 1893, and the two photos that survive of her as an old lady, show a bony woman with a prominent hooked nose and hooded eyes — even as a girl Kate Nichols cannot have been pretty. In later years she would be described as 'striking' with raven-black hair and flashing eyes, and 'an Italian look in which she rejoiced. She dressed to it in dark colours with splashes of crimson and orange' — but judging by her portraits the author of this description was flattering her.[7] There was a surplus of young women in her generation, and as a plain girl with strong opinions she would probably have struggled to find a husband. Lost or unrequited love became a theme that recurred throughout Kate's writings.

Despite her assertions that she was self-taught, there is some evidence that Kate did in fact have drawing lessons and also that she studied at the Norwich School of Art. In the interview in *The Bookman* Kate admitted to having had a talented drawing mistress at school. Apparently this mistress was a Miss Cartwright.[8] Charlotte Cartwright was the youngest daughter of a gunsmith who had extensive premises on Rampant Horse Street in Norwich. In 1861 she was working as a 'pupil teacher' at Norwich School of Art, but by 1871 she is listed as a drawing mistress, working by herself from premises in York Place. It may well be that Mrs Dunnett also had her give lessons at her school; parents probably paid extra for the privilege. Drawing and painting in watercolours were considered appropriate accomplishments for young ladies.

Miss Cartwright had been a student at the Art School, and won a prize in 1852 for 'an outline drawing from the flat' (that would have been a copy of a Roman or Greek frieze).[9] The prize was a silver medal. On the front was a bust of 'Victoria D.G. Regina'. On the reverse, 'Student Prize from the Department of Practical Art', the lettering surrounded by a laurel wreath. And that just about sums up what art education was in the 1850s — practical art, intended to fit artisans for the local industry or for jobs that required some degree of artistic ability. Other prizes were awarded for shading in chalk, drawings from the round (a drawing made from a cast of a Roman or Greek statue), geometrical drawings and shaded drawings of foliage and flowers. There was nothing remotely original or creative. Miss Cartwright would have been taught to copy, a skill rigorously enforced by the Art School — but it is reasonable to say that it was not 'art' as we would define it today. Rules of perspective were taught. Techniques in various media were taught.[10] But to imagine, to become bewitched by a scene, subject or landscape — to try to catch its essence — that was not on the curriculum. 'Seeing' was something you had to teach yourself by looking at pictures by other artists, by drawing endlessly and 'feeling' your subject. No doubt Miss Cartwright passed on to her pupils some of the rigorous techniques she had learnt, but given Kate's later praise of her she may well also have encouraged them to be creative.

The only evidence we have of Kate's early drawing is the sketchbook we mentioned in chapter 2. It includes several pencil sketches of Alton where her maternal grandparents lived, little watercolours and some rather clumsy paintings of flowers and leaves, and is dated 1859. Kate was twelve that year and the landscape sketches in particular show considerable promise. We looked at it,

18a. Pages from Kate's 1859 sketch book showing a view of Alton. Kate was 12 in 1859.

18b. Pages from Kate's 1859 sketch book.

along with her many other drawings, etchings and paintings that the museum keeps carefully preserved in acid free paper, and, under the watchful eye of the curator, turned over each page. One thing was immediately obvious: Kate's talent did not lie in figure drawing or flower painting but in landscape. A pencil sketch that she made of a river scene with figures and horses on the bank and clouds scudding across the sky, is very good indeed. The whole composition is dramatic and mature. When Marion was teaching art she says she would have been extremely pleased if one of her 12-year-olds had been able to capture the evocative nature of such a scene.

However, if you look to the right hand side of the same page, the figures sitting on the bank watching what is going on below them

19. Pencil sketch of a boy, possibly done at the Art School. The position and size of the right arm are anatomically incorrect.

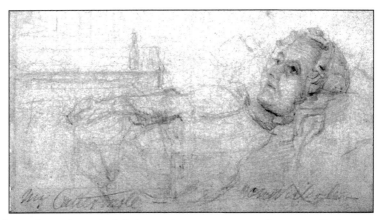

20. Pencil sketch of 'Mrs Cattermole'. The head is carefully drawn — but note the lack of any sense of the bulk of her body beneath the bed clothes.

by the river do not have the same life force. As we saw time and again in Catherine Nichols' paintings, etchings and drawings, although she was good at capturing the likeness and character of a person in a portrait, the rest of their body either did not interest her or she did not have the skill to depict it realistically.

After school, we understand Kate spent time 'in town' studying with 'Mr Kewan'.[11] This was actually David Hall McKewan, a water-colourist of some note and a member of the Royal Society of Watercolour Artists. He spent a lot of his time travelling around the country, but in the spring of 1871 the census tells us he was living with his sisters in Hampstead. He died two years later. We do not know when, or for how long Kate studied with him, or whether this study consisted of actual lessons or simply of visits by a determined and intense young woman to one of her heroes. No doubt she sought him out because in 1859 he had published a book, *Lessons on Trees in Water Colour* — and Kate, as we shall see, was passionate about trees. It may be that she had been given a copy of the book as a present. It is a beautiful volume, folio size and lavishly illustrated with pictures and details of trees, partly painted and fully worked up,

21. Pencil sketch from the Bosworth Harcourt collection. The figure is unfeasibly tall given the size of the head.

with details of the colours used for the different effects — Mr McKewan favoured combinations of Indian yellow, indigo and lamp black for foliage, for example. The sketches were made 'expressly for this work' and the colour reproduction is superb. 'The art of Printing in Colours has enabled the Publisher to place before the Student a Series of Lessons which cannot fail to be of great value; as each wash is given separately, and after in manipulation, it is believed it will be found to facilitate the Student in Painting Trees (hitherto one of the most difficult subjects in Water Colour Painting) more than a hundred pages of descriptive matter possibly could do, and in a short time enable him to paint a Tree that he may not only look on, but look into — one of the great beauties in Water Colour Painting' ran the introduction.

If Kate did indeed spend time with David Hall McKewan she must have done so in the late 1860s or very early 1870s as he died in 1873. It seems unlikely that her parents would have sanctioned such a visit before she came of age in 1868, though of course she did have relatives in London with whom she could have stayed and perhaps one of her cousins acted as her chaperone. In later years she would make a practice of descending, uninvited, on artists whose work she admired — she spoke of visits to Millais, to Lord Leighton and to Matthew Noble, the portrait sculptor.[12]

Finally, we know, she took a course at the Norwich School of Art in 1874. It seems rather curious that she left it so late — she was twenty-seven in 1874 and the local art school would have seemed the obvious place for an aspiring young artist to go much earlier in her career. It is tempting to see her enrolment as the result of Mr McKewan urging her to get some more professional training — but that is pure conjecture. Indeed it seems likely that she was actually at the school in 1875 not 1874. Few records survive from the early days of the School of Art, but a press cutting of December 1875 pasted into a scrap book tells us that 'Miss C M Nichols' won a prize — *Lives of the Italian Painters: Michel Angelo, by R. Duppa; Raffaello, by Quatremère de Quincy* — in the 'Advanced Division' for her work that year.[13]

Art education has changed greatly over the years. Any formal training that an artist received in the eighteenth century was most likely to have come from being apprenticed to a professional artist or craftsman or as a scenery hand in the theatre. Scenery painting, panoramas, dioramas, sign painting and other forms of decoration were the bread and butter of provincial artists — indeed, John Crome (1761—1821), one of Norwich's best known artists, started his career as a coach, house and sign painter, and his friend, Robert Ladbrooke (1768—1842), another Norwich artist, started out as an apprentice printer.

In the early nineteenth century Norwich was the home of artists who, by their common aims and close master–pupil and family ties, formed the only regional school of painting in England. John Crome and John Sell Cotman were its two great masters and in 1803 this loose knit circle united to found the Norwich Society of Artists, the first of many artists' groups that sprang up countrywide in the nineteenth century. From 1805 until 1833 they held meetings for artistic and intellectual discourse and annual exhibitions of their work. However, in the latter half of the 1820s Britain suffered an economic depression which had a severe effect on Norwich artists and was a contributory factor to the founding of schools of design. Patronage of the arts, ever at risk from economic fluctuations, had waned so much that in December 1830 the *Norwich Mercury* described Norwich as a city 'where taste is at so low an ebb that a public concert cannot find adequate support . . . a theatre cannot keep open for a few months'. The Norwich Society of Artists was disbanded three years later.

Many artists supplemented their incomes by giving lessons – the demand for private tuition from the emerging middle class was widespread by 1800. Jane Austen gives us a satirical glimpse of such pupils in her novels, poking gentle fun at her heroines: Marianne in *Sense and Sensibility*, who would, if given a fortune, 'have [had] every book that tells her how to admire an old twisted tree', Fanny Price in *Mansfield Park* who found it hard to tell the difference between water colours and crayons, and poor Catherine in *Northanger Abbey* who 'had no notion of drawing', thus falling 'miserably short of true heroic height!'

In Norwich, John Crome, John Sell Cotman and Robert Ladbrooke painted avidly for themselves, but to earn a living they had to teach, and teach a wide spectrum of the city – from genteel young women to merchants and tradesmen. John Crome was well known in Kate's family. He had taught drawing to her four Nichols aunts over a period of ten years at their home, Alpington Hall, and as he was a master at the Grammar School for a time he may also have taught her father and uncle. He was described by George Borrow in *Lavengro* as a 'stout little man whose face is very dark and eyes vivacious'. Most artists taught by getting their pupils to copy – Cotman had a library of what he called 'drawing copies' that he lent to pupils to work on between lessons or when he was unavailable to teach them – but Crome encouraged his pupils to 'let loose the reins of Taste and Fancy and to follow, unfettered, the course which their Imagination pointed out'.[14] Perhaps he took Kate's aunts out into the countryside to draw from nature as he did with many of his pupils. Perhaps they taught her in the same way and that is where her great passion for working outdoors was born. Sadly, Crome's ideas were well ahead of his time and although a fine artist and inspirational teacher, when he died in 1821 he was heavily in debt.[15] Some of Crome's paintings, along with ones by other members of the Norwich School, hung on the walls of the Nichols' home in Surrey Street and it is clear that they informed young Kate Nichols' ideas of what a landscape painting should look like.

The duties of an artist were not, however, restricted to engaging young ladies or gentlemen in artistic pursuits. His services were also required by a diversity of trades and professions needing someone who had the ability to draw and represent articles, designs and manufactured objects precisely. The artist/draughtsman had to be able to provide accurate representations for a surgeon, for an arms manufacturer, for an engineer, maps for military use, architectural plans and decorations. It is not surprising, then, that the first centres of artist training were heavily slanted towards trade requirements and pattern making.

Apart from the economic depression, a new invention also seemed set to deepen the difficulties of artists – photography. In 1826 a Frenchman succeeded in creating the first permanent image and in 1834 Henry Fox Talbot created permanent negative images using paper soaked in silver chloride. In 1837 Louis Daguerre created images on silver-plated copper coated with silver iodide and 'developed' with warmed mercury. With the fast developing ability of this new device to capture images that artists had previously produced, the importance of the draughtsman looked to be in jeopardy, though in fact it would be many years before photography really would supersede their work.

By the mid-nineteenth century, and particularly as a result of the poor showing made by English designs at the Great Exhibition of 1851, the government decided to set up schools of art and design in manufacturing areas to train designers to work in the local industries. In Norwich, John Barwell, an influential and gifted man, was ahead of the curve. He and his wife, Louisa, were passionate about education. He was a wine merchant and also a gifted amateur artist and a prominent member of the City Council. He subscribed to the contemporary belief that fine art could only be achieved if students had access to the great works produced by Greek and Roman sculptors, but money was needed to buy casts of these – and a permanent place had to be found to house them. Slavish copying of these works was at the heart of art school teaching. The schools concentrated on teaching accuracy and technique at the expense of creativity. Louisa and John Barwell disapproved of this approach and Louisa wrote a scathing comment on an exhibition held in Norwich in 1840. 'It has become too much a habit to consider the power to draw as a gift, as a mark of genius. . . . All persons may acquire linear drawing as readily as they learn to write.' In 1839 the Barwells established the first Norfolk and Norwich Art Union and revived the 'conversaziones' – what we would probably call 'private views' – where artists and art lovers met.

In 1840 – largely as a result of John Barwell's efforts – an exhibition was opened by him in the Bazaar in St Andrews. Its range, size and variety surpassed anything Norwich had seen before. From power looms, steam engines, a conger eel, Norwich shawls and daguerreotypes to a drawing exhibition in which were drawings entitled 'The Squint or Strabismus' and 'Crapean or Edible Frog'. There was a shooting carriage for an invalid, a cast of a deformed head and casts of club feet. The Victorian appetite for the bizarre and grotesque was admirably catered for.

However, both John and Louisa continued their fight for a proper art school and finally, in May 1845, Norwich Council granted a sum of £50 a year towards renting a space to house the school — and the city surveyor was employed to forward plans to enable the Bazaar, built in 1831, to become the art school. The sum was totally inadequate so John Barwell continued to pester anyone who was anyone in Norwich for donations and to join his subscription list. Finally, in 1843, Parliament granted £300 for the Norwich School of Design and appointed William Stewart as master. It opened in 1845. That November the *Norwich Mercury* carried an advertisement for the school. The opening hours were to be morning school from 9.30 to 12.30 at three shillings a month and evening school from 7 to 9.30 at two shillings a month and the branches of instruction were: classes for designing ornament; for drawing the figure with regard to ornamental design and classes for modelling. In June 1847, Frederick, youngest son of John and Louisa Barwell, won a prize at the school — the 'second class for the best outline drawing from the statue'.

From the beginning there were difficulties. The management committee was too large, the rooms were too cramped, manufacturers locally were dissatisfied with the training the school offered and in August 1847, William Stewart was dismissed.

This then was the state of art education in Norwich the year that Kate was born. Things did not improve radically under William Stewart's successors although there were some successes. In 1849, for example, the Norfolk and Norwich Association for the Promotion of Fine Arts held its first exhibition under the patronage of its President, Vice-President and the Council of the Norwich Government School of Design. It was a show of contemporary paintings and became an annual event — each one accompanied by a 'conversazione'. The School of Design thus became the venue for 'fashionable Society' which gave it a middle-class tone, but this inevitably undermined its stated function of improving industrial design. In the same year Norwich pupils gained more prizes than in any other school in the kingdom, as the *Norwich Mercury* proudly reported on 29th December 1849, though the majority of the prize winners were artistic young ladies rather than artisans. In the 1850s, under John Wilkinson Heaviside, the school became the Norwich School of Practical Design and enjoyed a period of comparative success.

But there were continuing financial problems and the school had too few pupils. The manufacturers who were supposed to benefit from the training the school gave their potential employees were dissatisfied. 'When the Norwich School of Design was established there appeared to be some promise of a direct benefit to the shawl manufacture, the only one of the staple trades in the town admitting to much scope for design' ran the Board of Trade report in 1849. It went on to say that there had been little contact and that now the connection between the School of Design and local manufacturers had all but ceased.[16] Further criticism followed. Students were ignorant of technical processes, a problem encountered not just in Norwich but in many schools of design. Lace designs in the Central School, for example, were described by Lady Trevelyan as 'absolutely impracticable and most of them useless . . . a total want of feeling for the material and manifest ignorance of the possibilities and requirements of lace designs'.[17] Extensions to the Art School — for which Norwich City Council paid £700 — rendered the building unsafe for some years and affected student numbers. The building also shared an entrance with the library which was highly inconvenient, and increasing numbers of students were taught off the premises.

Robert Cochrane was appointed head in 1859 and stayed until 1884. He was therefore still the head when Kate attended. By then the majority of the students were young ladies like Kate, who had, or believed they had, artistic talent. The reason was largely financial. In 1869–70, for example, the 94 male and female 'artizans' [sic] paid £44 16s in fees between them, while the 44 'ladies' and 9 'gentlemen' paid a total of £77 1s. Attending the Art School was rather like attending classes at an Adult Education centre today — students often only registered for one or two classes per week. By 1870 the fees ranged from 10s 6d a quarter for one afternoon session per week, to £1 6s for three morning sessions. There was no limit to the number of years you could spend as a student and each year's course in each subject led to an exam.[18] Students who would make their living as draughtsmen or artists or textile designers rubbed shoulders with the young lady hobby painters.

The Norwich School of Art was still not a particularly successful institution. On 28th August 1869 the examiners from South Kensington wrote a report to Robert Cochrane which began: 'There are no signs of improvement in this school' and it is clear from the few records that survive that over the next few years the school continued to perform badly. Years later, Kate Nichols would criticise the uninspiring teaching in English art schools ('South Kensington's cut-and-dried proceedings don't somehow attract the artistic soul') and gave that as the reason why she had left Norwich School of Art after just two terms.[19]

The Happy Eye records that the two most talented, prizewinning students in all of Cochrane's 25 years as head were Catherine Maude Nichols and George Skipper. It is a truly outstanding commendation. Kate was remembered as 'a formidable lady, a real gypsy of a woman, who was a great friend of my mother's, but alarming to me'.[20] George Skipper was at the school for just one year and became a renowned architect. He was to 'Norwich what Gaudi was to Barcelona'.[21] Both Kate and George were spirited and creative artists who felt there was little to be gained from the teaching a provincial school of art could provide.

But however much Kate despised the teaching at the Art School it seems likely that it was there that she learnt the technique of etching which would later serve her so well. Her first known etching is dated 1875 — the year she was at the school — and is a Norwich scene entitled 'College'.[22] She may not have attended classes in etching — she claims that she was never taught how to use a burin and it is unlikely this was an outright lie — but it is very probable that she saw other students' etchings and learnt from them. According to Joan Banger's notes, made from documents in Norwich Library that were destroyed in the disastrous fire of 1994, 'Miss Nichols remembered with gratitude valuable information she obtained from Charles John Watson.'[23] Charles Watson produced his first etching in 1869 and they were fellow students — perhaps he taught her the technique.

22. 'College' dated 1875. This seems to be Catherine Maude Nichols' earliest known dry-point.

5

Etching

Kate Nichols worked in a whole range of different media. She produced oils and watercolours, miniatures and pencil sketches, but, though she would have preferred to be known as a painter, she was most successful as a printmaker. Perhaps it appealed to her as a way of making her work available to a wide range of people, though it was certainly much more labour-intensive and less spontaneous than painting or sketching. It may help readers to appreciate her work more if we give a brief description of the print-making techniques she used. The fact that she was so good at dry-point and etching — both meticulous and time consuming processes — may also give us some insight into her character.

'It is a gift,' she told readers of *The Women's Penny Paper* in 1889. 'Some grand painters can't etch a bit. Some etchers have no eye for colour. It requires decision. You must have the "courage of your opinions" to etch well. Hesitation is fatal. Then you must be able to express a great deal with a few lines and must pay attention to values. That is why I like it; there is more of the soul of art to a minimum of manual labour.'

Most of Kate's prints were dry-points. Dry-point is the easiest of all print-making techniques and, put simply, involves scratching a design into a soft plate with a sharp implement. In Catherine Nichols' day, plates were usually made of copper or zinc and creating the design required steady hands and strong wrists — Kate claims she inherited these characteristics from her surgeon father. Today's print-makers sometimes use plates made of plastic or even specially prepared card which are obviously much softer to work. Any implement made of a substance harder than the plate can be used to make the design; Kate would have used specially produced steel or diamond-tipped needles called 'burins' which were available from art shops. The 1880s saw a revival of interest in the technique and an increasing number of dry-points were produced. Confusingly, they were often called 'dry-point etchings' and the technique was often described as 'etching' when in fact it is more properly a form of engraving (true etching involves drawing a design on a metal plate through wax and using acid to bite the lines from which the design will be printed — see below). However, in this volume we too will use the contemporary term 'etching' to mean 'dry-point etching'.

First Kate would have had to de-grease her metal plate with a mixture of salt, vinegar and whiting (which she would have had to prepare herself) until no droplets

of water gathered on its surface when it was wetted; this was to ensure that it did not repel the ink. The design would then be engraved into the surface of the plate through a tracing of an original sketch, or it could be drawn directly on to the plate if she felt sufficiently confident of her draughtsmanship. The technique requires a degree of physical strength to force the needle through the metal and this affects the end result — lines tend to be short and straight or with very simple curves, and scoring parts of the plate heavily could produce areas of rich black. Viewed closely, the lines tend to look rather scratchy and by varying the direction of the scratches it is possible to create an impression of movement or even turmoil — something Kate used to good effect in her images of the windy Norfolk countryside.

The special characteristic of dry-point is the 'burr' — the metal gouged out of the engraved lines — which forms a mound on either side of the groove. If left in place, this burr holds the ink and prints to give a distinctive feathery or velvety appearance. The amount of burr produced depends on the angle of the engraving tool — a perpendicular angle will leave little or none while the smaller the angle of the tool to the plate the larger the burr. A talented engraver would vary the angle of the tool to produce different effects for different areas of the picture and wipe away the burr where a clean line was required. The deeper the engraved line, the more ink it will hold and the wider and blacker it will print. Because in a dry-point the end result depends so much on the quality of the burr, comparatively few prints can be taken from the same plate without loss

23. Detail of dry-point.

of quality. With each printing the burr flattens out or rubs off so each print in a run will be slightly lighter in colour than the last and the lines will lose more and more of their texture.

Inking and printing are the messiest part of the process and it seems that Kate did not often undertake this herself. A handful of her prints are inscribed 'Printed by the artist' — which implies she probably did have a printing press in her studio — and some are inscribed 'Printed by the artist and D. Hume'[1] but she told interviewers[2] that her printer was 'Mr Goulding of Shepherds Bush'. He was Frederick Goulding (1842–1909). As a 15-year-old he was apprenticed to Day and Sons in Lincoln's Inn Fields and it was soon clear he had a talent for the work. By the 1860s and 70s he was producing prints for many well-known artists, including Whistler, Samuel Palmer, Alphonse Legros and Seymour Haden, founder of the Society of Painter-Etchers. In 1880 he set up his own business with three printing presses at Kingston House on Shepherds Bush Road, and in 1893 he also acquired a lithographic printing press. There were printers in Norwich but Kate Nichols chose the best she could afford.

Printing ink is black and gooey and has to be spread liberally over the plate, forced down into the engraved areas and then scraped off with bits of cardboard and wiped off the smooth areas with pieces of scrim, taking care not to disturb the burr. The work surfaces and the printer's hands would have become stained and the ink would have got under their nails and on to their clothes. Next, the edges of the plate had to be bevelled with a fine file to prevent them cutting the paper on which it was to print. Finally, the inked plate could go into the press, face up under a sheet of wetted paper and sandwiched carefully between more sheets of paper and protected by layers of blanket. The press itself would have been large and heavy, rather like an old fashioned mangle, and turning the handle would have been heavy work. It is easy to see why Kate chose to hand over this part of the process to the professionals, but there were disadvantages in doing so. The plates had to be sent from Norwich to London and there was always the risk that they would be damaged in transit. Unless Kate was present in the studio she would not know how the finished print looked and whether the plate needed re-working in any way. And printing was not cheap. In 1904 Mr Goulding charged Rosalind Birnie Philip, Whistler's executrix, three guineas for 25 artist's proofs, for example.

Kate Nichols also produced genuine etchings. Unlike dry-point, this process allowed numerous copies to be produced from the same plate without loss of quality, and this was how she illustrated her books and produced folders of printed work for sale. Etching involves a metal plate coated with wax through which the picture is scratched with an etching needle. The plate is then placed in a bath of acid which bites through the lines scored in the wax to create a picture from which an image can be printed. These days there are all sorts of health and safety issues about the use of acid and consequently etching has fallen out of fashion, but in the nineteenth century there were no such problems and it enjoyed a good deal of popularity. Nonetheless it was a messy and potentially dangerous technique although it is much easier work than dry-point and enables the artist to produce much more fluid lines and curved shapes.

Blocks of etching wax are commercially available today but Kate Nichols would have had to mix her own — 40% beeswax, 40% asphaltum (a sort of bitumen which is now called 'Gilsonite') and 20% powdered colophony resin (from pine trees) melted together for a 'hard' ground and the same mix with added tallow for a 'soft' ground. It was an unpleasant, smelly process. When fully mixed the concoction was taken off the heat and allowed to set into blocks.

24. Detail of an etching.

Even then there was a lot to do before Kate could begin drawing her picture. First a metal printing plate had to be de-greased using the mixture of salt, vinegar and whiting described above. Then the clean plate was heated and when it reached the required temperature a thick smear from one of the wax blocks was applied. This had to be spread evenly over the plate with a leather 'dabber' and the plate then had to be removed from the heat with a spatula — newly waxed plates are too hot to handle. Only when it was cool could she begin to draw her design with etching needles of various thicknesses and scrapers to remove larger areas that she wanted to print in solid black. It is a lot less effort to engrave a design through wax than to incise it into the plate but it is less easy to see how the design is progressing and to gauge how it will print.

When the first stage of the design was complete the plate had to be immersed in a bath of nitric acid diluted in water. Again, Kate would have had to buy her own 'aqua fortis' from the chemist and dilute it further — the usual ratio is 1 part acid to 10 of water. Nonetheless, even at that dilution, acid is dangerous stuff. Sliding the etched plate into the acid had to be done very, very carefully — any splashes would have burnt her hands and there were no acid-resistant latex gloves available for her to wear as there are today. She had to be equally careful as she 'feathered' the surface, stroking it gently with a swan's feather to remove any bubbles from the surface of the plate. No doubt she collected the feathers on walks along the river bank and stored them in a pot alongside her acid bath. With use, the acid gradually turned them a bright chrome yellow. She had to gauge how long her etched plate should remain in the acid bath; this depended on the size of the plate, how deeply she wanted it etched and the temperature in her studio that day because that affected how fast the acid would bite into the metal. From time to time, no doubt, she removed the plate and examined it to see how the etching was progressing — risking acid burns each time. Etchers were known for the scars on their fingers. When she was content that the plate was sufficiently etched it had to be washed, the wax had to be removed with turpentine and she again had to bevel the edges of the plate before printing from it.

Etching is a tricky medium and most plates would have required numerous trial printings and sessions of re-working. This meant that Kate herself probably undertook some of the inking and printing processes described above — at least of the trial proofs — though she would have despatched the completed plates to a printer for producing prints in quantity. Although etched lines are less soft and painterly than lines in dry-points, they can be more fluid, and the great advantage was that unlike dry-point plates, etched plates could be used many times without the quality deteriorating — some of Kate's print runs of etchings ran into the hundreds. There were 350 editions of her folder of etchings commemorating George Borrow's centenary, for example.

On occasion Kate also produced lithographs — Norwich Castle Museum has some she did of Stranger's Hall. 'Litho' comes from the Greek for stone, and the process involved printing from a highly polished block of Bavarian limestone. The image was drawn on the block in something greasy like wax or crayon, then the stone was coated with a weak solution of nitric acid and gum Arabic which would eat into the parts of the stone not covered by the design and form a water-retaining layer of calcium nitrate salts. At that point the stone was sent off for printing — either to Mr Goulding or to a local printer. The stone would be wetted and the etched areas would stay damp and repel the printing ink, a special concoction based on linseed oil and pigment-laden varnish which would seep into the waxed or crayoned areas. The excess drawing material would then be wiped off with lithographic turpentine and the stone would be put through the press.

There were various types of lithography — chalk lithography, using a type of crayon, mezzotint style, which involved covering the whole stone with lithographic grease and wiping areas away with a soft cloth, lithotint which meant painting the stone with washes of lithographic ink of varying degrees of intensity and so on, but Kate seems to have stuck to the most straightforward method, often known as 'pen and ink' lithography.[3] This meant drawing on the stone with a pen — or a brush for large areas — and a special type of greasy fluid. This was almost as easy as sketching except that Kate had to be sure not to rest her hand on the stone as the grease from her hand would make a mark that would print and spoil her picture. Colour lithographs could be produced using a separate stone for each layer of colour — the technique lends itself to large areas of flat colour and was particularly suitable for posters — but Kate's prints always seem to have been in black and white. Like etching, lithography allowed more freedom of expression than dry-point and had the advantage that there was no limit to the number of impressions that could be taken — but though she produced a number of lithographs in the 1890s, Kate seems to have tired of the experiment and returned to working in the medium with which she was most familiar.

Frederick Goulding's business closed in 1904. By then Kate Nichols had plenty of printers to choose from nearer home — the 1901 *Eastern Counties Directory* lists 29 in Norwich alone — but she seems mostly to have sent work to Jarrolds. They certainly produced her folder of etchings *After Crome* and the one she produced for the George Borrow centenary, and earlier in her career they had published her books of stories and poems.

25. Detail of a lithograph.

6

'Painting all day long'

In the course of her lifetime Kate Nichols produced a prodigious quantity of work, much of which survives. There are three significant collections in Norfolk — one in the Castle Museum, a collection of (mostly local) prints in the Local History section of the Millennium Library in Norwich and a collection of drawings and sketches in the Norfolk Record Office. There is a further collection of over 50 of her pencil drawings in the Ashmolean Museum in Oxford and some etchings in both the Victoria and Albert Museum and the British Museum. In addition there is a large body of her work in private hands and works by her are still coming on the market at regular intervals, as a quick Internet search will reveal.

She experimented with various subjects but the vast majority of her work falls into one of three categories: landscape, townscape and seascape. There are a handful of portraits, she painted a few miniatures but we have not found any examples, and from time to time she drew interiors. Some of her work is dated but the majority is not, and as her subject matter did not change greatly in the course of her lifetime and there is very little in the way of progression in her style of working, creating a coherent timeline of her work is something of a challenge. Fortunately she was a frequent exhibitor and exhibition catalogues, where they exist, are the most useful tool we have for charting her travels and what she produced when, though sometimes it is like trying to fit together a jig-saw puzzle in which half the pieces are blank or completely the wrong shape.

We know she exhibited one work at the Royal Society of Artists in Birmingham, one in Dudley in the West Midlands, nine at the Walker Art Gallery, Liverpool, two at Manchester City Art Gallery, just one at the New Gallery in London (Kate's work was probably too traditional to sit well alongside that of the pre-Raphaelites and members of the Arts and Crafts movement), four at the Royal Society of British Artists in Suffolk Street, and ten at the Royal Society of Women Artists. She showed work at numerous other galleries in London, including the London Salon and the Royal Academy. She sent works to exhibitions in Paris, Venice, Munich, Melbourne and St Louis — but this is just a list of places and numbers and we do not know what she actually showed in these various places.[1]

The two organisations with which she exhibited most regularly, the Royal Society of Painter-Etchers and the Norwich Art Circle, will be dealt with separately, but there are a number of other exhibitions about which we do have useful information. Between 1877 and 1908 Kate exhibited a number of works in the Royal Academy Summer exhibitions,[2] nearly all of them prints. We know the titles of the works and copies of most of them survive.

Exhibits at the RA

Date	Title
1877	'Rue des Cordonniers, Dives'
1878	'Falling leaves, Barbizon'
1879	'Ber Street, Norwich'
	'The thicket'
	'Unlading'
1882	'A Norfolk Broad'
	'Street in an old coaching town'
1883	'Old houses, Norwich'
	'Cow Hill, Norwich'
1888	'Riverside, Norwich'
1889	'Evening on the Broads'
1891	'Strangers' Hall, Norwich'
1908	Unknown

In May 1892 she held a one woman show entitled 'Gleanings by Woodland and Wave', first at the Stacey Gallery in London's Bond Street and then at a gallery in the Royal Arcade, Norwich. There were 150 exhibits in a variety of media. The critic in the *Bury and Norwich Post* singled out a work called 'The corner of a field' as proof of 'how deft a mistress of foliage she is', but he was less impressed by her seascapes — 'of her oil paintings she is happier when the gleanings are by Woodland rather than by Wave. The sea is an exacting mistress,' he continued, 'and not to be wooed, or at any rate won, by a hasty glance,' and he criticised some of her Cornish seascapes quite harshly. But he liked her landscapes. 'Contrast these [seascapes]', he wrote, 'with "A Norfolk Dyke", "Wandering Waters", "An old City Court", "Up a Court at Cley", two of "Mousehold Heath" and "A Norfolk Broad" which are excellent and characteristic examples of East Anglian scenery. . . . The same defects and excellences may be seen in her water colour drawings.' He listed the titles that particularly pleased or displeased him before moving on to 'Her dry point etchings are excellent examples of her fascinating art; two companion pieces "Amidst the Pines" and "Skirting the Wood" are admirable. . . . The collection . . . testifies alike to the talent and industry of this clever East Anglian lady.'[3] A mixed bag of comments but an invaluable compendium of titles of works she had produced by 1892.

A catalogue survives of another exhibition, this time one she held in the Queen's Hotel, Manchester.[4] It is undated but her address is given as 73 Surrey Street, so it must have been after 1900 and probably after 1911/12 as that seems to be when she visited Jersey and Somerset and views of both places are listed. The exhibition contained 18 oil paintings; most were of Norfolk scenes but one was entitled 'Taunton trees' and one was a portrait of 'P. E. Sewell Esq.' There were three watercolours — 'Surrey trees', 'Lourdes' and 'Castle Orgueil, Jersey', and a group of etchings and pencil sketches. There were also some Cornish ones, a version of the etching of Rue des Cordonniers that Kate had shown at the Academy in 1877, views of Montreuil, Rheims and a French chateau, a picture of Dickens' House and a scene in Bristol. Finally there was a little group of miniatures, some of which were portraits but several were landscape views.

While Kate undoubtedly had talent, some of her success was due to the fact that her father, and later she herself, had money. It also helped that she was resourceful, adventurous and had a great deal of self-confidence — it never seems to have occurred to her that she might not be made welcome wherever she went. While other artists scrimped and struggled to meet or study with their heroes — Kate just got on a train. She enjoyed sketching and painting out of doors and when she heard there were artists at Barbizon doing the same thing, she simply travelled to France and joined them.

The original Barbizon painters — Jean-Baptiste-Camille Corot, Jean-François Millet, Théodore Rousseau, Charles-François Daubigny and their followers — had been inspired by the paintings of John Constable to paint landscapes from nature. By the 1840s several of the group had settled in the little village of Barbizon in the Forest of Fontainebleau. Millet introduced the idea of also painting the people who lived in the landscape, faceless peasants engaged in backbreaking toil; probably his most famous example of this genre is 'The gleaner', painted in 1857. For a while the 'Barbizons' were seen to be doing something genuinely new and different, but by the late 1860s, going out to Barbizon to spend time painting in the forest, perhaps actually meeting some of the founder members of the group – Rousseau and Millet lived there until their deaths in 1867 and 1875 respectively – and generally having fun was a popular activity for young artists studying in Paris. It was these young artists that Kate Nichols later described to her friends. Amongst them, at various times, were Monet, Renoir, Sisley and others who would go on to found the movement we know as Impressionism – but we cannot say whether they were among the young men Kate met. Indeed, she does not really seem to have met anyone. She told the *Women's Penny Paper* that 'some hundreds of artists were distributed through the village. I was painting all day long, and did not get to know any of them – being wrapped up in my art – and only coming into contact with them at the table d'hote where I was treated with as much deference as I could desire. They were of all nationalities.'[5]

It would seem she visited Normandy in late 1876 or early 1877 and she had certainly been to Barbizon by the summer of 1878, but we have no way of knowing whether she made separate visits to Normandy and Barbizon, or one visit that took her to various places in France. All we know is that she exhibited an etching entitled 'Rue des Cordonniers, Dives, Normandy' at the Royal Academy in 1877 and the following year she exhibited an etching of 'Falling leaves, Barbizon'.[6] By the mid-1870s the original 'Barbizons' were all dead so she would never have met the great men who founded the movement. If she was aware that she had arrived rather too late to be a part of the main action, she kept quiet about it.

26. *'Chateau near Paris' by Catherine Maude Nichols. Dry-point.*

Instead she made the whole episode sound quite thrilling, which no doubt it was for the carefully brought up girl from Norwich. She said she was the only young woman there, staying in a run-down chateau for the bargain price of twelve francs a week which included a huge ground floor room 'full of black caricatures', five meals a day — and a dance with free punch thrown in on Sundays! The house was full of reckless young men, fooling about and making a lot of noise, she was woken each morning by someone blowing a French horn and a black horse would often put its head in through her open bedroom window. At night the exuberant young students would go out and light fires so they could study the effects of light. The woods around Fontainebleau were full of snakes and the young men all wore buskins to prevent them from being bitten[7] — we do not know what Kate wore on her own feet but she told the *Penny Paper* that she wandered through woods where there were snakes and wolves, following lines of blue arrows marked on the trees to avoid getting lost.

But her trip to France gave her a taste for travel. In or before 1879 she took herself to Newlyn in Cornwall, a small fishing village near Penzance. The village is picturesque and the granite cliffs rising out of the sparkling sea are spectacular. Penzance was relatively easy to get to by rail from London and when you got there, accommodation was cheap. Throughout the 1880s artists flocked to Newlyn — by 1884 there were at least 27 resident in the village and numerous others visited. Like the 'Barbizons', these were people who wanted to work from nature, to paint dramatic landscapes and picturesque cottages, to draw 'characters' who were still living lives untouched by the industrial revolution. These artists would come to be known as the 'Newlyn Group', and their acknowledged leader was Stanhope Forbes. This time, Kate Nichols was at the forefront of the trend and as early as 1880 she exhibited an etching of 'Pilchard boats at Newlyn'.[8] Kate liked Cornwall and visited on a number of occasions so it is difficult to know which of her many stories relate to her period in Newlyn — but it may well be the one about renting rooms from an old Cornish widow and sitting painting at one end of the kitchen table while her landlady prepared their meal at the other end. The sleeping arrangements were equally Spartan: 'I think I lay on the floor, I know we climbed up a sort of ladder at night and had but one candle, stuck in a bottle.'[9]

There would be other visits. The writer of the article in *The Women's Penny Paper* who visited her in her studio in 1889 says, 'I was struck by a series of drawings executed on the Cornish coast, including a very beautiful sea sunset, with the light of evening shining through a breaking wave.' Unfortunately it is not clear whether these were recent works, meaning Kate had visited Cornwall again in 1888–89, or ones from the earlier visits.

Kate told friends about how she would go pilchard and mackerel fishing with the locals 'on a moony night' and wake in the morning in her rented cottage to find the fishermen's wives had left her presents of freshly gutted fish, and about how she lived in a cave with 'Nature's earth for a floor . . . for months on end'; this latter was probably something of an exaggeration. There was the story of how

27. 'Cornish street' by Catherine Maude Nichols, 1879. Dry-point.
Exhibited at the Norwich Art Circle in 1888.
Reproduced by kind permission of the British Museum.

she got lost one night on the moors and had to strike inland for fear of falling over a precipice in the dark and was eventually rescued by a 'peasant woman' with a lantern on the end of a long pole. On another occasion she climbed part

28. 'Ruined barn' by Catherine Maude Nichols. Oil painting.
Reproduced by kind permission of Sarah Colegrave Fine Art.

29. 'Old buildings' by Catherine Maude Nichols. Oil painting.
Reproduced by kind permission of Sarah Colegrave Fine Art.

way down a cliff at Kynance to sketch with her drawing equipment 'nailed' to her – then found she was stuck and couldn't get back. Again, she was rescued by locals with ropes and a pole 'plus much expenditure of muscle on her own part'.[10] One gets the impression that the people of Cornwall must have spent a lot of their time keeping an eye on the foolhardy young artists who had arrived in their midst! No doubt they were generously rewarded for their pains. Kate obviously relished these adventures and dined out on them for years amongst her more conventional friends back home.

In the mid-1880s she visited France again, this time Lourdes and the Hautes Pyrenees. By this point she had become a Catholic and no doubt this gave special significance to the visit and to the shrines and caves she drew. None of these pictures survives but a series of them was exhibited at the Norwich Art Circle and the Society of Painter-Etchers in 1885/86/87.

Other etchings show that she went further afield: 'A Chateau near Paris', two women in an alleyway sitting in the sun which may be of Spain or Portugal, a town in Germany, a view of Bruges. She was adventurous but, though she did travel extensively, the vast majority of Kate Nichols' surviving work is of Norfolk and Norwich.

She loved quaint, tumble-down old buildings. At the presentation of her portrait to the Castle Museum in 1923, Prince Duleep Singh recalled that Kate 'adored Norwich, with all its surprising picturesqueness, and she deplored every modern effort to destroy its beauty for the sake of mere convenience. If ever she heard that any old world lane or corner was threatened with destruction she at once made an etching of it so that at least future generations should know how beautiful Norwich had been.'[11] A number of these appear in a book of stories, which she both wrote and illustrated, called *Old Norwich – or Second Fiddle* published by Jarrold and Sons in 1886. A list of the scenes in the book – all meticulously captured – gives some idea of her work: Wickhams Yard off King Street, Elm Hill, St John's Alley, Magdalen Street, St Anne's Wharf and another view

30. 'Riverside, Norwich' by Catherine Maude Nichols, c.1886. This shows the river in a peaceful light. Oil painting.

of King Street. She also left a record of 'the spectacular fire that occurred at Messrs Ranson's timber-yard by the side of the Wensum some years ago'.[12] It would seem that as news of the fire spread, Kate packed up her sketching things and headed off to the riverside, heedless of the possible risk to herself — or the inconvenience she might cause the firemen trying to get the blaze under control.

The Millennium Library collection of her work is in the Local History section and from that it can be seen

31. 'Dutton's Court' by Catherine Maude Nichols. Dry-point. This seems to have been a 'best seller' — numerous copies survive. Reproduced by kind permission of the British Museum.

32. 'Tombland' by Catherine Maude Nichols. Dry-point.

just how much more of Old Norwich she captured. 'Dutton's Court seen from within', a Norwich river scene from Foundry Bridge, 'George Borrow's house on Willow Lane', 'Old houses, Riverside', 'Norwich Guildhall', 'Ber Street', 'The Bethel Hospital', 'Cow Hill', several views of what is now the Roman Catholic Cathedral of St John, 'A Norwich courtyard', 'Old houses on King Street', 'Old house, Tombland', 'Norwich Castle', 'Butchers Alley' — and many others not identified. She has left Norwich a valuable record of courts and corners of the city that have long since disappeared.

Also from this collection we can see some of the other places she visited: Great Yarmouth, Beccles, Caston, Whitlingham, Wymondham, Eel Mill, Thorpe, Carrow Point, Earlham, Wroxham, Somerleyton, Mundesley Dell, Acle, Ipswich, (King's) Lynn, Brancaster, Lakenham and many unidentified places — windswept dunes and seascapes, wooded hills, broads, marshes and endless trees.

33. 'Brancaster Staithe' by Catherine Maude Nichols. Dry-point.

34. 'Wroxham' by Catherine Maude Nichols. Dry-point. Note the use of line to suggest wind and movement.

35. 'Dunes' by Catherine Maude Nichols. Reproduced by kind permission of Sarah Colegrave Fine Art.

And all of this work was undertaken without a motor car, travelling by train and on foot and carrying with her whatever equipment she needed on any particular trip. She had a determined dedication to her art; discomfort would never prevent her from capturing a particular scene or feature of wild weather — indeed, in some ways she seems to have relished it. Looking at the windswept sea scenes gives some idea what this must have been like for a Victorian lady in long skirts and hat — probably firmly pinned to her head with vicious hatpins. Norfolk artists still paint the wild coastal scenes. In March 2014 the 'Norwich 20' group

36. Martin Laurance sketching in Norfolk in a high wind — just as Kate would have done.

37. 'Seagulls over Orford Ness' by Martin Laurance.

38. 'Beccles' by Catherine Maude Nichols. Dry-point. Note the rather strange composition with the buttressed wall dominating the right hand side of the image and the empty foreground.

of painters celebrated its 70th year with an exhibition in the Millennium Library. One of the exhibitors was Martin Laurance, and the photograph of him painting one of his exhibits captures for us just what it must have been like for Kate.

Looking at hundreds of Kate Nichols' drawings, etchings and paintings, two things stand out above all else: the isolation and loneliness in so very many of them, and the wild movement of waves and the wind in trees and grass in others. Only the beautifully observed, drawn and etched images of old Norwich have a sense of stability — and even then they are tinged with isolation and emptiness. There is never any sense of Norwich as a lively, vibrant city full of people — partly, no doubt, because Kate was still not good at drawing figures.

Another characteristic of her work is that the foreground is often empty. The eye is led in to find something of interest in the distance — down the hill, across the river, a building just glimpsed through the trees. Sometimes the interest is completely hidden but we are led to imagine there will be something to see just round the corner if we follow the path through the woods, or cross the bridge, or take the winding track over the hill. We wondered whether this was part of Kate's psychology (in her writings the life to come is always incomparably better than life today) or was it a format she particularly liked, or simply the result of something more prosaic, like long sight or some other visual defect? We began to

39. 'Steep narrow street' by Catherine Maude Nichols. Dry-point.
Reproduced by kind permission of the British Museum.

40. 'Trees and road' by Catherine Maude Nichols. Dry-point.
Reproduced by kind permission of the British Museum.

realise that, compositionally, much of her work is very close to that of many of the Norwich School artists[13] whose paintings she had known since childhood. The empty foregrounds are Kate's own idiosyncrasy, but all the artists, and in particular, John Crome (1768–1821) and George Vincent (1796–1831), painted endless pictures of tracks disappearing into woods, houses half hidden in the trees, rivers meandering away out of sight. Like Robert Ladbrooke (1769–1842), Kate often favoured vistas where the eye is led to a village or a building far off on the horizon. Her work was particularly similar to that of some of the younger members of the Norwich School — for example, her interest in quaint details and forgotten corners mirrored that of Henry Ninham (1796–1874) who created meticulous paintings, drawings and etchings of Norwich townscapes, and many of her landscapes are very similar to those of John Joseph Cotman (1814–78), one of John Sell Cotman's sons, though his use of colour was much more assured. These men were older than Kate — they were coming to the end of their lives as her career was beginning — but given the nature of Norwich society it is quite possible that she may have met some of them.

Inevitably, with Norwich and Norfolk as their subject matter, many of Kate's paintings and etchings depict the same places, the same picturesque buildings, the same wide vistas across the Broads and the same views of the Norfolk coast as those painted by the artists of the Norwich School. Sometimes the similarity is almost uncanny — for instance, some pencil sketches by John Sell Cotman

41. 'Reeds' by Catherine Maude Nichols.
Dry-point.

of 'Boats on Cromer beach'[14] could be the model for those in Kate's images of 'Oulton Broad', the graceful curves of the clinker built fishing vessels are lovingly delineated by them both (see plate 47).

Other of Kate's pictures concentrate on detail almost to the exclusion of the background — a patch of grass, pebbles on a beach, a clump of reeds. Sometimes items of interest only reveal themselves after careful study. In one pencil drawing in the Ashmolean, for example, there is an object in the sky which at a casual glance might be taken for a bird. On closer examination it is obviously too big to be a bird and when viewed carefully, through a magnifying glass, it turns out to be a bi-plane.[15] Like so much of Kate's work the sketch is undated, but even at the

42. Copy of a pencil sketch by Kate Nichols in the Ashmolean Museum, Oxford. The speck in the sky on the right hand side of the picture is actually a biplane — see detail.

time of her death in 1923 planes were a comparatively rare sight. It is therefore curious that when one appeared over a scene she was sketching she relegated it to such an insignificant role. She may, of course, have felt it was an unfortunate example of modernity intruding on nature — but if so why did she not simply miss it out?

She commented in her article in *The Women's Penny Paper* that she could not really separate drawing and poetry and hardly ever painted a picture that did not have its 'duplicate in rhythm' in her mind: the movement of words and rhythms was there when she saw movement in trees or waves, and certainly some of her poems reflect this close harmony. The second verse of a poem called 'Dance of the leaves' illustrates this very clearly:[16]

> *The tune that they dance to sounds high in the air,*
> *And no choice have these dancers to whom they shall pair;*
> *Pale yellow and orange, sienna and brown,*
> *They flutter and rustle and flit up and down,*
> *List, list to the dance of the leaves.*

It could perhaps be said that only an artist would use the word 'sienna' to describe the colour of leaves — and the use of the archaic word 'list' may suggest someone who struggled with modernity. Kate was also a fan of the poetic title, particularly for her later work. An etching in the 1915 Norwich Art Circle Black and White exhibition, for example, was labelled 'The savage rock that circling mists enfold', a watercolour of 1920 was entitled 'Life's old cottage, battered and decayed/Lets in new light through chinks that time has made' while a watercolour of trees she exhibited in November 1922 was called 'Where lacey films the leafage dark o'erspread'.

Although the vast majority of Kate's works were etchings or drawings she did also work in colour. 'I prefer oils to any medium but watercolour insists on being used for some subjects' she told the interviewer from *The Bookman* in 1913. Several of her oils and water colours show how well she could handle those media — something she perhaps learnt by seeing the work of other artists in Cornwall or Barbizon and working with them. However, not all her watercolours are so successful and on at least one occasion the Norwich press referred to her 'dingy delight in watercolour'[17] suggesting that clear fresh colours were not part of her usual repertoire.

Certainly she was most successful as a printmaker. Etching had become popular in the middle years of the nineteenth century, enabling artists to produce multiple copies of their work — something that probably appealed to Kate's sound

43. 'Sheringham' by Catherine Maude Nichols. Watercolour.
Reproduced by kind permission of Mr and Mrs M. Emery.

business sense. Asked why she etched she replied that it was 'a gift'. Not everyone could do it. And she said she liked the fact that it was possible to evoke so much movement and feeling into a work with so few lines.

44. 'Sheringham' by Catherine Maude Nichols.
Watercolour. Reproduced by kind permission of Mr and Mrs M. Emery.

45. 'Sheringham' by Catherine Maude Nichols.
Oil painting. Reproduced by kind permission of Mr and Mrs M. Emery.

The writer of the article in the *Women's Penny Magazine* likened her to Meryon. Kate was duly grateful — she seems to have considered such a comparison a great compliment, but given his career trajectory it seems to have been a rather back-handed one. Charles Meryon was born in Paris, his father being an English physician and his mother a French dancer. After his mother's early death he entered the French navy and made a round-the-world voyage. He was already a draughtsman and on the coast of New Zealand he made pencil drawings which he was able to employ, years afterwards, as studies for etchings of the landscape of those regions. His artistic instinct developed; when he left the navy, having found that he was colour blind, he determined to devote himself to etching and entered the studio of the engraver Eugene Bléry. Meryon had no money so had to undertake boring work copying for artists to earn a crust, but he was also beginning to do original work of his own, notably a series of etchings. Though highly valued amongst other artists, his work never sold well in his lifetime and he ended a sad life in a mental institution, penniless, in 1868. Too late he was to become recognised as a superb etcher; in 2014 a print of his which had originally sold for a cent fetched $1,000 in an auction in America.

One of Kate's proudest achievements was becoming a Fellow of the Society of Painter-Etchers — later the Royal Society of Painter-Etchers. She was probably encouraged to join them by Charles John Watson who seems to have been a fellow student at the Norwich School of Art. He was a near neighbour of the Nichols, the son of a painter and gilder on The Green, and Kate's exact contemporary – they had probably known each other since they were children. He began by working for his father, mixing colours, but he was successful in building a career as an artist and etcher in his own right.

The Society of Painter-Etchers was founded in 1880, the brainchild of Seymour Haden, a surgeon and talented amateur etcher.[18] On 31st July he and five friends, Heywood Hardy, Hubert Herkomer, James Tissot, Alphonse Legros and Robert Macbeth styled themselves 'Fellows' of the fledgling society, and that December they were joined by two others, Philip Gilbert Hamerton and Edward Hamilton. In the spring of 1881 they organised an open exhibition for etchers and engravers 'for the purpose of demonstrating the then state of the art in this country, and ascertaining whether the material existed for the formation of a Society having for its objective its further promotion'. The response was overwhelming. Not all the works submitted could be hung but there were a huge number of exhibitors. Charles John Watson from Norwich was one of them and Kate was another. We can only imagine the thrill and sheer excitement she felt of being in London amongst artists from England, Europe, America and Canada. Kate had family in London, but she chose to stay in a boarding house in Marylebone for the duration of the show.[19]

In the catalogue artists are not listed in alphabetical order, but Kate is on the first page and she had six etchings in the exhibition: 'Rue des Cordonniers' (4 guineas), 'Ber Street Norwich' (4 guineas), 'The thicket' (3 guineas), 'Unlading' (5 guineas), 'Charing Cross Norwich' (2 guineas), 'The forge' (3 guineas). Her first two sold. The most expensive item in that first exhibition was a work by Tissot – priced at 10 guineas.

All the exhibitors seem to have been invited to become members of the Society – including 18 of the foreign artists.[20] We also know that after the exhibition, described as 'a test exhibition', a letter was sent to all those who had become 'members', stating that to become Fellows of the Society they had to submit a work which would be judged on merit by the committee members, and those thought worthy would become 'Fellows', but it also seems that some 69 of them were elected Fellows straightaway.

The submission procedure was implemented the following year, 1882, at what the Society rather confusingly described as its 'First Annual Exhibition'. Ten Fellows were elected, of whom Catherine Maude Nichols was one. She had submitted an etching of a group of Scotch firs – very similar, in fact, to the Scotch fir that appeared in David McKewan's book on drawing trees – and one of 'Crown Point'. The committee chose the fir trees. Kate subsequently and confidently

46. 'Scotch firs'. Dry-point. This is the 'Diploma Piece' that gained Catherine Nichols her
Fellowship of the RSPE in 1882. Reproduced by kind permission of the British Museum.

asserted that she was 'the first lady Fellow', a claim that is frequently repeated, even by the Society itself, and she was indeed the first woman to be elected on the basis of diploma work.

In an article in *The Studio* in 1907 the correspondent writes:

> The etchings of Miss C M Nichols have long been familiar to visitors to the exhibitions of Painter-Etchers, of which Society for 10 years she remained the only Lady Member. She has found many of her subjects in Norwich, which is her home, and her art expresses very ably the character of the streets of that old city. But the etching of Oulton Broad, which we reproduce, is an example of her sense of style and gift for understanding the true qualities of the etched line.

Note this article describes her as a member rather than a Fellow, adding to the confusion. Was there in fact a distinction or by then were the two terms interchangeable? The minutes are not at all clear.

In a number of other interviews Kate would also claim to have been the 'only lady Fellow' of the Society for some ten years. However, Seymour Haden kept an example of each 'diploma piece' submitted with a note of the year the

47. *'Oulton Broad' by Catherine Maude Nichols, illustrated in* The Studio *in June 1907. This was exhibited at the Norwich Art Circle Black and White Exhibition in 1887 and is illustrated in the catalogue.*

individual was 'elected' and that collection (1880–1909), together with some of the documentation, is now in the Ashmolean Museum in Oxford and clearly shows the quality of work that entitled someone to become a Fellow.[21]

The collection contains 69 works from exhibitors to the 1881 'all-comers' exhibition including those by two women. They were an etching of 'Young Bacchanals' (a group of naked cherubs) by Dorothy Tennant, and a view of 'Goose Pond' by Mary Nimmo Moran. Not all the exhibitors of 1881 are represented in the collection so some selection process was at work; were these people 'Fellows' or simply members whose work Haden saw as in some way exceptional? Certainly the catalogue of the 1883 exhibition describes Mary Moran as a Fellow, presumably on the basis of 'Goose Pond' as there was no diploma piece submitted by her in either 1882 or 1883. So does that in fact call Kate's claim into question? Did Mary Moran and Dorothy Tennant actually become Fellows before her?

There are Fellows' diploma pieces from each subsequent exhibition — a handful each year, sometimes a dozen, more often only two or three. If there is uncertainty about whether Dorothy Tennant and Mary Moran were members or Fellows, there is none about the later submissions which are clearly labelled. They show that Edith Berkeley and the Countess Feodora Gleichen were among the three Fellows elected in 1884, Elizabeth Adele Armstrong and Elinore Hallé were among the thirteen elected in 1885, Lilian Hamilton, Victoria S. Hine and Anna Lea Merritt were elected in 1887 and Ethel King Martyn and Elizabeth Piper's diploma pieces were accepted in 1892 — making at least nine other lady Fellows in the first decade of Catherine Nichols' membership! So, whether or not she was the first lady Fellow, she was certainly not the only one for ten years. This is not in any way to minimise her achievement. It really does not matter whether she was the first, or one of the first, the only, or one of very few ladies to become Fellows of the society — to be one of ten (or possibly twelve) lady Fellows among nearly 100 men was no mean feat. But what is significant is that it was so important to Kate. She was hugely competitive in an almost masculine way and was desperately anxious to maximise her success by emphasising its uniqueness — even if that meant bending the truth. It is an interesting aspect of her character.

The Royal Society is now at Bankside, next door to Tate Modern, and we arranged a visit there to look at the early records. In a tiny cramped back room, filled with old prints, casts of heads, books, a computer and precious little space to look at or open anything, the very helpful curator brought out the original catalogues. They were small brown covered books about 10 x 14 cm. No illustrations, of course, such as we would expect today, but they did list the works exhibited, the artist and what was being asked for each work. (The Society got a percentage of the price of any work sold).

In 1884 the annual exhibition was held in Liverpool and Kate did not exhibit — perhaps because they wanted to take 25% of any sales. But she did show work in 1885. This time the exhibition was held in the Egyptian Hall, Piccadilly. The 1886 exhibition was held at the Corporation Art Gallery, Derby, probably because Seymour Haden had a family connection to the city. Kate had obviously visited the Pyrenees as two of her works that year were 'Betharram, Haute Pyrenees', and 'A Southern Village, Haute Pyrenees'.

The 1887 exhibition was back in London in Bond Street in the new galleries of Messrs Dowdeswell. The papers were not impressed and described the rooms as 'dark and therefore unsuitable for work requiring close examination'. And, of course, prints do need to be closely examined. It is noticeable that the price Kate was asking for her works had dropped very considerably from that first exhibition in 1881. In this one she had two unframed prints at a guinea each and one at 10s 6d.

After a somewhat peripatetic start, in not always ideal conditions, 1888 ushered in a new era for the Society, and Haden — the life force of the Society of Painter-Etchers, albeit to the discomfiture of many of its members due to his overbearing and strident personality, and in particular to his dislike of his brother-in-law, the renowned artist, Whistler — was able to report that year that he had made 'gracious communication' to Her Majesty and had requested that the Society had now reached sufficient status to warrant the conferring of 'Royal' to its name. It has to be added that this was due in part to his overriding desire to get equal with Whistler who had managed to get a royal charter the year before for the Society of British Painters of which he was President. The art world does not seem to have been a particularly friendly place! In an attempt to smooth over the years of wrangling, in 1889 the Royal Society of Painters and what was by then the Royal Society of Painter-Etchers agreed to share the same exhibition space — 5a Pall Mall — where they remained until 1938. Fellows could now add 'RE' (Royal Etcher) to their names — and Kate Nichols made sure that she always did so. It is notable that, even in her childhood sketchbook, Kate signed or initialled virtually everything that she produced, however slight.

The 1917 and 1918 catalogues make very sad reading indeed. Not surprisingly, in 1917 there were many more women than men listed as exhibitors, and several men who had work exhibited did not live to see it hung. Lieut. Alick Gornall and Lieut. Luke Taylor are recorded as 'Late'. The 1918 catalogue is dominated by works reflecting the terrible time the men had lived through — the titles a snapshot of the war: 'Circumstances of war', 'Morning calm', 'Battle cruisers off Jutland', '13th Flotilla leading the battle cruisers', 'The ramparts', 'Homewards', 'Bois de Trone 1915', 'German trench and strong point destroyed', 'Before evacuation', 'Landing at low tide' and 'War workers', this last by a woman, Janet Simpson.

Kate, however, made no change to her choice of subject matter. She had three works in the 1917 exhibition and two in the 1918 — one was of Swainsthorpe, a village a few miles south of Norwich, the others were of trees and landscape.

Kate continued as an active member/Fellow of the society, taking part in annual exhibitions well into the twentieth century. Some of the catalogues have unfortunately been lost or damaged but she was still exhibiting in 1919. Two of her works were included that year — 'On the Broads' and 'The Old Manor at Stiffkey'. They were her last recorded exhibits with the Royal Society of Painter-Etchers to which she had, rightly, been so proud to belong. Although she was listed as a Fellow in the 1920 catalogue, no works are included and she was already suffering from the cancer which would kill her two years later.

But involved as she was with the Royal Society of Painter-Etchers, Kate still found time to be an active member of her church and very much a part of the artistic community in Norwich, as we shall see in the following chapters.

7

'Sub conditione' Catharina Maria Nichols

Eighteen-eighty-two was a memorable year for Kate Nichols. It was the year she was elected a Fellow of the Royal Society of Painter-Etchers — and it was the year she was received into the Catholic Church.

On 21st November 1882 Kate stood in the little chapel of St John Maddermarket. Father Bede Wrigley tipped some Holy Water over her head, then dipped his thumb into a small bowl of the Oil of Chrism and gently crossed her forehead, uttering the timeless words, 'I Baptise thee . . .' in his lilting Irish accent. As she had already been baptised into the Anglican Church as a baby (on 5th November 1847), the words 'sub conditione Catharina Maria Nichols' were added to her Baptismal certificate.[1] Both the water and the oil Father Bede used would have been prepared and blessed at the previous Easter Chrism Mass. There was no

48. Copy of the entry for Catherine Nichols in the Register of Baptisms at St John's.
Note the mis-spelling of her surname.

49. St John's Maddermarket. This was the Catholic Chapel where Kate was baptised. It is now the Maddermarket Theatre.

elaborate ceremony, no warm family presence. Her sponsors would probably have been there and possibly some close friends — but there is no known record of them.

The Catholic Chapel was first built on the west side of the churchyard of St John Maddermarket in 1794. It was a rather ugly, squat, serviceable red brick building — having nothing to recommend it from the outside. In 1835 the land in front of the chapel came up for sale and the Catholics bought it and added a school room and a more attractive entrance with an arch surmounted by a cross. But if the outside was plain, the inside was full of colour and light and was beautifully decorated — especially at Christmas when garlands hung from the gallery rails which ran right round the church and housed the organ loft. The name tags that can be seen on the seats in old photographs would indicate that worshippers gave a donation to the church for their chosen seat.

When the chapel was converted to a theatre in 1921 — there being no further need for it since the magnificent church of St John the Baptist had been finished and opened — the cross over the arch was taken down and replaced by a mermaid. However, that too was taken down during the second world war as a safety precaution in case of air-raids.[2]

At a future date, probably fairly soon after her baptism, Kate would have gone to Confession and attended Mass there, in Latin of course, and received, amongst fellow Catholics, the Holy Sacrament for the first time from Canon Duckett, or his curate at that time, Reverend William J. Wyke, though she would not have received wine — only the wafer. Wine, or the Blood of Christ, was not given to the congregation — only the priests received it. The Vatican changed that ruling in 1960 and now everyone is offered both the blessed wine and bread though not everyone accepts the wine.

We do not know what made her decide to become a Catholic and we have no sure way of finding out. There are several possibilities. She lived opposite the Catholic Convent in Surrey Street. Could she have been influenced by the nuns? Had she met Father Bede Wrigley through them? Father Bede seems to have been a somewhat itinerant Franciscan priest with a passion, and talent, for making converts. He was used in this role by the church and was also the governor of retreats in London, Glasgow, Chilworth, Bristol and Liverpool. It was in Liverpool that he so impressed a Miss Imrie and her aunt that they both became Catholics, being accepted into the church by him at Bolton. Miss Imrie later became a nun and finally an abbess. She also funded the building of the Friary Church in Liverpool as, having been to Rome and seen the glorious churches there, she wished to provide something of that splendour for the poor of Liverpool.[3] But in 1882 Father Bede was attached to Canon Duckett in Norwich and is listed as a priest at the Maddermarket.

Or could Kate have been influenced by other Catholics, her Italian friend Elisabetta Marcantonio for example? Or did she know the Barwells who had lived in Surrey Street for many years? John Barwell and his wife Louisa were Catholics — and extremely influential in the city in business, art and education. John Barwell was a fine artist himself having first exhibited with the Norwich Society of Artists when he was just fifteen and had a portrait that he painted of Florence Nightingale's aunt exhibited in the National Portrait Gallery in London in 1868.[4]

50. Photograph of Canon Duckett, Kate Nichols' friend, spiritual mentor and an important figure in late nineteenth-century Norwich.

Perhaps she was first attracted to Catholicism by Canon Duckett, the charismatic head of the Catholics in Norwich and a leading figure in Norwich who was on the board of governors of the Art College in 1876 when she was there for one term. He was widely admired in Norwich as a wise but warm and humorous man with no 'airs or graces'.

It could simply be that Kate was caught up in the spirit of the time in the same way that many other free-thinking intellectuals were, but we do know from her obituary in the Eastern Daily Press that it was not an easy decision. She 'went through a period of great spiritual unsettlement and anxiety, whence she escaped by taking refuge in what she conceived to be the traditional fortress of authority'. Debate about religion was rife in the nineteenth century. The Church of England was the church of queen and country — but non-conformists had already persuaded many in those congregations to join them. At the time of the Census of Religious Observance in 1851, most village chapels had larger congregations than the local Church of England parish church. Perhaps many village clergy had become too complacent, too much in the pocket of the local squire and not in real touch, or empathy, with farmers and labourers. Kate's friend Mary E. Mann wrote many stories which point to this. In one of them a farmer says of the local parson, 'to think that eighty pound o' my money — hard-earned and scraped together — go year by year to keep that weak and pappy idiot to talk his d---d trash from the pulpit'![5] The same attitude was rife in towns and cities.

By the middle of the century the great intellectual debate about Catholicism versus the Church of England, which had been vigorously re-opened by John Henry, later Cardinal, Newman, had drawn many intellectuals to the Roman Church. But it also had another effect that is not always remembered - the anxiety felt by many Anglicans that the parish church was no longer at the centre of people's lives and imagination. Uncertainty was in the air. First non-conformity had asserted itself and now there was the growing threat from Catholicism. For many this was deeply disturbing.

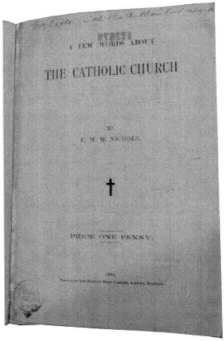

Intellectual argument for 'pure faith', as voiced by Catholics, led to raucous and often vicious public exchanges — in which Kate took part, often a lone female voice, for religion was, and always had been, a male-dominated territory. A pamphlet[6] which can be seen in the Millennium Library in Norwich was written, and published, by her in 1885 — and is extraordinary. It begins:

> The Catholic Church is an
> indisputable fact existing in
> the world.

51. Title page of A Few Words about the Catholic Church by Catherine Maude Nichols.

> *There are few civilised men who have not at least heard of Her; as Her*
> *reputation may be justly considered widespread. Other sects may reign in*
> *certain localities, as the Anglican Church in England and some colonies;*
> *the Wesleyan in certain parts of England etc. When we consider that there*
> *are in the world 200,000,000 Catholics to 130,000,000 Protestants we are*
> *considering a fact that contains much content for reflection.*
>
> (1)   *How did this Church originate?*
>
> (2)   *What supports an institution so contrary to the natural bias of*
> *men's prejudices?*

The Catholic Church was, and still is, dominated by male clergy – and for a
lay member of the congregation, a recent convert and a female one at that – to
publicly set forth the beliefs of the church was unheard of. Even more unusual
was that after she had written it – and before she had it printed – Kate sent a
copy to Canon Duckett to make sure that the content was correct – and then
printed her letter and his reply at the front of her tract. He wrote politely that
her description of accepted Catholic belief was correct – though perhaps not
expressed 'as he would have done'. Whether she asked him for permission to use
his reply we don't know, but it caused uproar and the local press had a field day.

Publishing such letters in the press was not new. Writers, some of whom
preferred to remain anonymous, had, as early as 1824, written articles or letters
with inflammatory titles. Reverend C. J. Smyth contributed *Anti-Catholic Pills to
Prevent the Gripes of Conversion*. 'Anonymous' set forth a moral tale called *Cats
let out of a Scarlet Bag – or Pussies Caught in a Protestant Trap* in 1844. By 1852
the tone was more serious. Reverend John Jephson wrote *Observations on the
Practical Tendency of the Roman Catholic System*. Then, in 1885, came *A Few words
about the Catholic Church* by C. M. Nichols. Of all the letters and tracts in the
Millennium Library collection hers is the only female voice. Fifteen letters were
published after the publication of her tract; she had stirred up a hornet's nest
in Norfolk. Some supported her, many were against; most concentrated on the
disparate views of 'souls', 'spirits', 'saints' and 'angels'. She responded politely but
vigorously in two published letters with excellent arguments written with style
and flourish, ending the second one, 'I don't write for controversy but to make
you see what we do. I shall write no more on the subject.' The editor too had
had enough of this particular subject and after her final letter added the rather
patronising comment, 'We willingly allow our correspondent the final word. It is
a lady's privilege.'[7]

The dark and forbidding towers of St John the Baptist Roman Catholic
Cathedral still dominate the skyline of Norwich, dwarfing local houses and inns,

and Kate did many drawings and some paintings of it — some of which were printed in *The Great Gothic Fane*, a book which was published in 1913 in celebration of the church. The towers are square, more like a castle or fortress, and have none of the grace and beauty of the spire of Norwich Cathedral that pierces the city skyline, pointing towards heaven. In contrast to the outside, however, the inside of the cathedral is full of space, tranquillity, colour and exquisite decoration. Kate must have loved it and would have watched its building with both interest and excitement. The events that led to the building of the church began well before Catherine became a Catholic and by the time she was baptised in November 1882 it had already reached an advanced stage of preparation. The foundation stone was laid on 17th July 1884. Practically all present were invited guests, led by the Bishop of Northampton, Dr Riddell. Interestingly, among those present (as listed in *The Great Gothic Fane*) was Father Bede OSF, the same priest who had baptised Kate. Ten years of building were then to pass by before the completed nave was opened for use and so replaced the two existing Catholic chapels, including Kate's beloved St John's Maddermarket. On 29th August 1894, the Feast of the Beheading of St John the Baptist, 'the Nave was solemnly opened — this time with all ceremony and éclat'. There can be little doubt that Kate would have been among those present at that service.

Two important events had happened in 1877 as far as the Cathedral was concerned.

Canon Richard Duckett came to Norwich in 1876, the year of the great devastating flood that November, as head of the Catholic Chapel in Maddermarket, though there was a powerful Jesuit mission in the city as well. He was 43, in the prime of life and bristling with energy and ideas — of which the building of a magnificent church in Norwich was the main one. He came from an old knightly Catholic family which had settled in Westmoreland in the time of Richard II and had continued to support the Catholic Church. Two of his ancestors had been martyrs to the cause — the Venerable James Duckett in 1602 and his grandson, the Venerable Father John Duckett in 1644.

> *You shall return to prison* [(Newgate) — declared the judge in 1644] *and taken from prison, placed on a wicker hurdle, and dragged to Tyburn, where, you shall be hanged with a rope, and when you are half dead your heart and bowels shall be taken out and your body divided into four parts.*[8]

The memory of these horrific events must have remained in the family.

On arriving in Norwich, Duckett immediately involved himself in every aspect of the city's life, especially education and provision for the poor of the city. For ten years he sat on the Board of Guardians, for three years he was Chairman of the Relief Committee, and it was a common question with the anxious poor who went seeking relief, 'Will Dr Duckett be at the meeting today?' For 25 years he was Governor of the Norfolk and Norwich Hospital and the Jenny Lind Infirmary. For many years he served on the Committee of the Eastern Counties Asylum of Idiots and (in stark contrast) that of the Norwich School of Art. In fact he was a member of nearly every society and institution in Norwich concerned with the poor and suffering. One might have expected the Bishop of Norwich, leader of the Anglican Church in the locality, to have been at the forefront of these concerns, but it was Duckett. He was the man who was most admired in Norwich. As a priest and preacher he was respected and listened to: as a man and a citizen he was honoured and loved.

As head of the Catholic community he would certainly have known Henry, the 15th Duke of Norfolk — a member of a wealthy Catholic family. The Duke was devoted to the task of bringing Catholicism back into the centre of British life and had already been a prodigious benefactor of the growing Catholic communities throughout the country, building churches, schools and convents. Duckett turned to him — describing the great vision that he had — and asked him for financial support for the building of a magnificent church. This was a project that chimed immediately with the Duke's own passionate interest.

The second significant event of 1877 was the marriage of the Duke to Lady Flora Abney-Hastings. At that time, the few Catholics that there were in Norwich used the chapel they had built next to the Church of St John Maddermarket (now the theatre) or the Chapel of St Peter and St Paul in Willow Lane. The Duke was more than happy to help — it would be his gift in thanksgiving for the happiness he was sure that his marriage to Lady Flora would bring to his life. Sadly that happiness was short lived. Lady Flora died a mere ten years later, before any of the church had been completed, having given birth to just one son who was born blind, mentally handicapped and epileptic. She died before the boy's eighth birthday.

52. The 15th Duke of Norfolk, who was largely responsible for building St John's Church, now the Roman Catholic Cathedral.

Canon Duckett and the Duke set to work. The site for the new church was purchased from Norwich City Council in 1879 and the

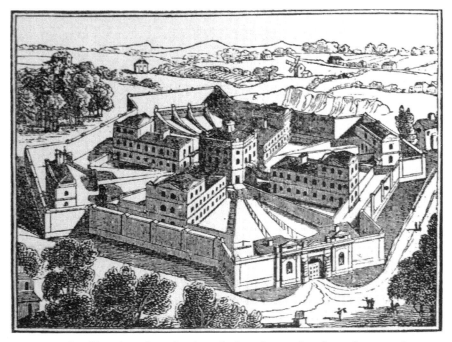

53. The Old Gaol. St John's Church was built on the site where this gaol once stood.

first sod was cut on the feast day of the Beheading of St John — a sombre event in keeping with the site on which the church was to be built — the old city prison. The gaol had only recently gone out of use — the last prisoner to be executed from there was hanged at Norwich Castle in 1867, a 22-year-old man who had killed his uncle, he was executed on a Monday to stop voyeuristic crowds gathering. Gradually society was becoming more civilised and realising that public executions were barbaric. After 1868 they would cease to be performed in public.

The construction of the church was beset by difficulties and really was only completed at all because of the inspiration and tenacity of Canon Richard Duckett and the benevolence of the Duke. The work had started and was well under the way when disaster struck.

The architect George Gilbert Scott the younger was appointed the architect in 1879 — a significant choice, for as well as being an established architect, in 1880 he himself became a Roman Catholic, to the shock of his family. Scott was born in London on 8th October 1839. He was the eldest son of Sir George Gilbert Scott, also an architect, and his wife, Caroline, née Oldrid. After a scholarship to Eton College he began training at his father's office. In 1866 he obtained a degree in moral sciences at Jesus College, Cambridge. During the 1860s and 1870s he worked for his father in his architectural practice and in 1872 he married Ellen

King Sampson. As well as designing St John the Baptist Church in Norwich he was also responsible for buildings in three Cambridge colleges, Christ's, Pembroke and Peterhouse, the main buildings of Dulwich College, the churches of All Hallows, Southwark (1877) and St Agnes, Kennington (1880) (both of these sadly destroyed by bombing). His residential work in the Queen Anne revival style is found in the Avenues area of Kingston-upon-Hull. Much of his work was in this style or in imitation of late Gothic architectural styles.

After his father died in 1878 George Gilbert Scott became distanced from the architectural business, and lived off his inheritance. Later he was placed in Bethlem Hospital; a petition by his brothers and his wife resulted in him being found of unsound mind in a public examination in 1884 but he escaped to Rouen in France, returning to England in 1885. He was confined to hospital again in 1885 and 1891–92. He died on 6th May 1897 from cirrhosis of the liver whilst in residence in the hotel at St Pancras station, designed by his father. He was buried on the 11th May 1897 at Hampstead. He did not live to see the completion and opening of his last work, the magnificent church he had designed in Norwich. George Gilbert Scott's design and the work he had started was carried on by his brother, John Oldrid Scott, who was immediately faced with a severe problem. Medieval chalk mines beneath the site were discovered as work began, and these had to be secured, resulting in two full years' work before the foundation stone could be laid in 1884. Furthermore, ten years into the project, it was discovered that the stone used (Beer limestone from Devon) was not weathering well, and it was decided that the remainder of the construction should be carried out using Ancaster stone from Lincolnshire. There are three forms of Ancaster limestone but the architects chose the one known as Hard White — which is just what it is. It had been widely used in stately and important buildings like St John's College Cambridge, built in the early sixteenth century. The magnificent interior of St John the Baptist's church shines with the whiteness of this stone and it was excellent for the intricate carvings which adorn the entire building.

As if that wasn't enough the Duke, embarrassingly, discovered that they did not have permission to complete the church to the full length specified by the architect. He applied to the City Council for further land to be made available to complete the church. No land was available, they said. Permission refused. In 1892 he wrote very long and brilliant letter, which survives in the archives of St John's Cathedral.

> To The Worshipful Mayor of Norwich
>> Dear Mr Mayor — After considerable hesitation I venture to address you on the subject of the church I am building at Norwich.

As you are aware, difficulties have arisen as regards the length to which I am entitled to extend the church. . . .

The Duke insisted that he had not known that the church was too long and that the Corporation had only now brought it to his attention. He went on to list all the difficulties and the potential loss to the city of a magnificent building:

. . . I have now, however, built half the church and I do not think any member of the Corporation will suggest that it is a building of which Norwich has any cause to be ashamed. We read in history that the last Duke who lived in Norwich left in a huff because the city authorities forbade him to have trumpets blown before him in the streets. I fear you may think the present Duke is trying to blow his own trumpet. . . .

He denied this of course, and the letter continued at length extolling the great beauty of the architect's designs and work:

Norwich has got half my church. If it does not want the other half perhaps I had better build it in some place that will appreciate it more . . . I had really hoped the old city would be proud of what would have been . . . the most beautiful example of pure Gothic to be found in England. . . .

The Duke continued by setting out all the problems the Corporation had listed and hoped they could come to a 'friendly and common sense solution'. He ended:

I have the honour to be, my dear Mr Mayor, your obedient, humble servant.
NORFOLK

The Council capitulated. Building continued.

The nave of St John's consists of ten bays, supported by massive cylindrical columns. It is 160 feet (over 49 metres) long and 60 feet (18 metres) high. The ten bays are supported by massive cylindrical pillars made of Frosterly marble. (54. Interior) This beautiful and ornate stone has been quarried in the North Pennines at a place called Frosterly, near Weardale, since the twelfth century. It is a special type of limestone which is fossil rich. Although known as 'marble' it is technically just limestone that has been subjected to extreme heat or pressure, or both, and has marine fossils from 325 million years ago embedded in it. The earliest known reference to it is in the Bolden Book — a northern version of the Domesday Book made by Bishop Hugh de Puiset in 1183 — through the entry

54. *Interior of St John's Cathedral, 2011.*

55. *Watercolour of St John's Cathedral by Kate Nichols, produced especially for* The Great Gothic Fane.

56. *Pencil sketch by Kate Nichols with St John's in the background. Published in* The Great Gothic Fane.

'Lambert the Marble Cutter'. The most famous use of the marble can be seen in Durham Cathedral where the ceiling of the chapel of the Nine Altars is supported by slender columns of this breathtakingly beautiful stone. In that great cathedral the columns would have been roughly hewn in the Frosterly quarry then transported to Durham where the monks would have had the hugely laborious task of rendering them smooth by polishing them with sandstone, leather and water. Perhaps the architects of St John the Baptist church in Norwich wanted to emulate the earlier magnificence of Durham Cathedral in their church —

continuing, in their minds, an unbroken line of Catholic worship.

Also of note are the great number of attractive sculptures and some of the finest nineteenth-century stained glass in Europe, in particular the windows of the Sunken Chapel, or the Chapel of St Joseph, for they depict Saints Flora, Pauline, Esther and Barbara (the four names of the Duke's first wife, Lady Flora Abney-Hastings). The Duke later married Lady Gwendolyn Herries who bore him a son and three daughters. She added the chapel in the north transept whose windows depict the story of the shrine at Walsingham.

Kate was probably present on 28th August 1894 when the nave, Baptistry and Memorial Chapel were opened and used for Mass and other ceremonies, and she must have watched as work continued unabated on the rest of the church; no doubt she also attended other key moments in the church's development.

A milestone was reached in 1906. That year marked the Golden Jubilee of Canon Duckett's priesthood and his 30th year as head of the church in Norwich. A solemn High Mass was celebrated with priests attending whom he had known since boyhood. At Benediction in the evening the church was again crowded, and later the Lord Mayor of the city presided over a huge event in St Andrew's Hall which was attended not just by churchmen and women, but by the citizens of Norwich. There was a musical programme with works especially composed, and an address from the Sisters of Notre Dame Convent. Many members of Canon Duckett's family were there, and the fitting climax was the reading of a telegram sent on behalf of Pope Pius X sending a very special blessing to Canon Duckett for the services he had rendered to the Church over the many years of his priesthood.

At length the great day dawned when the impressive church was complete and the opening ceremony could be celebrated. It is perhaps fitting that the date chosen was 8th December 1910 – The Feast of the Immaculate Conception. But a great sadness would mar the triumphant ceremony. Canon Duckett, the prime mover in getting the church built, died on 7th July 1910, just a few short months before the opening. His enormous standing in the city was evident. The streets were thronged for his funeral procession. Many poor people who were not Catholics but had benefitted from his loving and hardworking interest stood in the street to honour him. Many members of his family were there. Although a man of high honour in the Catholic Church – he had received the seldom awarded Papal Medal – he had obviously not separated himself from his roots. There were many high ranking members of the Anglican community in Norwich as well who revered him for his obvious goodness. He was not a pompous man. Intelligent, fearless, hardworking, imaginative and driven by his faith in the service of God and man – he always kept his feet very firmly on the same ground that everyone else trod.

The 4th Bishop of Northampton, Dr Keating, officiated at the opening ceremony which was also attended by the Duke and Duchess of Norfolk and the Mayor of Norwich. In his opening speech to the congregation, the Bishop said 'this is no ordinary church . . . the majesty of its architecture, the vastness of its spaces, the endless charm of the mighty pillar, soaring arch and triumphant vault . . . recall the masterpieces of the Ages of Faith and challenge comparison with them'.

Just two years after it opened, in 1912, St John's was the venue for the 3rd National Catholic Congress, a great honour for the Catholic community in Norwich for by this point

MRS. VIRGINIA MARY CRAWFORD.

MRS. FRANK ST. AUBYN (MARY RORKE).

MISS COLOGAN.

LADY EDMUND TALBOT.

LADY WINEFRIDE ELWES
From drawing by Mr. J. S. Sargent, R.A.

MISS C. M. NICHOLS, R.E.

MISS ETHEL ST. BARBE.

MISS FORTEY, B.Sc.

57. Roman Catholic ladies of Norwich. Kate Nichols is bottom left.

they were lucky enough to have the largest parish church in England, and it is from accounts of this in *The Third National Catholic Congress Norwich 1912*[9] and *The Great Gothic Fane* published in 1913 that we can see just what a significant part Kate took in the life of the church, and how important it had become for her. Her photograph (a very unflattering one) appears in *The Great Gothic Fane* as one of the eight leading ladies in the church.

Already very active in the world of art in Norwich, she threw herself into work in the church and contributed several etchings and two water colours which she painted specially for the book. The frontispiece, a water colour, shows St John's from Chapel Field North and it is followed immediately by one of the stained

58. *Strangers' Hall, where Canon Duckett lived for a time. Lithograph by Catherine Maude Nichols, 1886. This image was exhibited at the Norwich Art Circle in 1889.*

glass windows in the Chapel of our Lady of Walsingham. Also printed are Westgate Street with All Saints in the distance, St Peter's Hungate, Carrow Abbey and the staircase in Strangers' Hall (this is significant as for a time Canon Duckett lived there).

The crowning event of the 1912 Congress was a pilgrimage to St Walstan's Well, Bawburgh, in which over 500 people took part. There is a photo in *The Great Gothic Fane* and Kate may well be amongst the great queue of women patiently waiting though the photos are not clear enough for us to recognise her.[10] The Pilgrimage was headed by a pre-Reformation crucifix from Costessey Hall, the seat of an ancient Catholic family a few miles from Norwich, and many drank from the well and took water away with them in bottles thoughtfully provided by the organisers. A sketch that Kate made can be seen in the Millennium Library — but it is dated 1882 so she did not make it on this particular visit.

The books *The Great Gothic Fane* and *The Third National Catholic Congress* make clear just how much practical work was organised within the church in helping Catholic communities and poor people throughout the country. The

59. *'St Walstan's Well'. Dry-point. Kate drew this on a visit to the shrine in 1882.*

books contain a list of every society and all their activities. The Catholic Truth Society and the Catholic Federation were both well established and run by the clergy and men. In this meeting, the Catholic Women's League — for voluntary work in relation to the church — was established. It was to be for 'Apostolic Service'. After an opening address by the Bishop of Northampton a paper entitled 'Women and Civic Duties' was read. Women from London, Manchester and other towns and cities took part — and so did Kate: 'Miss Nichols, Norwich, participated', records *The Great Gothic Fane* on page 241. Many other 'leagues' were listed, most of them being run by men, but another which featured largely women was the Catholic Stage Guild which tried to steer dramatic art away from 'baser things' and to provide help to Catholics involved in the theatre in finding support wherever they were travelling to perform and to keep them in touch with their faith. There was a Needlework Guild, a Social Guild, an association for the care of crippled children and another for the protection of young girls. There was also a Social Association. Kate is not mentioned directly in any of those and indeed it is difficult to imagine her as a member of any such formal, conventional organisations.

For the three days that the National Congress took place, St John's must have been full to bursting with clergy and lay members from all over England. Frederick Hibgame, a life-long lover of Norwich and a Catholic convert, was there and wrote an account of it which brings to life something of the splendour and excitement that Norwich experienced:

> No one who was fortunate to be present in St Andrew's Hall on that night when the Lord Mayor of Norwich, in full state, welcomed His Eminence the Cardinal and nearly the whole of the Catholic Hierarchy, can ever forget the scene ... a Cardinal wearing sacred purple, attended by a dozen or more bishops in full insignia and literally hundreds of other dignitaries and priests made a blaze of colour ... No Catholic who heard those hundreds of voices singing 'Veni Creator' and 'Faith of our fathers' could help being touched. I thought of the grand old Dominican Friars, thrust forth from their glorious Church at the will of that most despicable of all English monarchs. ... The whole scene was such that I, who have known Norwich all my life, certainly never expected to witness. When I look back on the Norwich of 40 years ago and its two poor chapels and scant evidences of Catholic life and compare those days with our own ... to see our glorious new St John's packed from end to end with people brought from all parts of England and Ireland, Scotland and even America ...

He wrote a great deal more, but even this short extract from his description gives us a contemporary view of the enormous effect the completion of the church had on Norwich. And it was really all down to Kate's friend and mentor, Canon Richard Duckett.

She was certain to have been in the congregation during all the important ceremonies described in minute detail in *The Great Gothic Fane.* She would have rejoiced at Canon Duckett's Jubilee celebrations, perhaps sitting by her friend Mrs Radford Pym who is listed as having been there. She would have surely wept at his funeral. She had watched the great church being built. She had attended Mass — often celebrated by Canon Duckett — almost every week since she had joined the Catholic faith; she had attended the Third National Congress held at St John's and mourned again that Canon Duckett was not there to take part.

Her poems give us some clue as to just how essential her faith was to her. Her life had been so full and yet so demanding. Never an easy person, simultaneously racked by doubt and completely sure of her own opinion, it is to be hoped her faith gave her hope and some serenity in the later years of her life.

Peace at Death

> And, as the ruffled surface of a lake
> While winds torment it, will refuse to take
> Within its peaceless depths and image there
> The pictures formed around by nature fair;
> Yet will, when winds at eve have fall'n to rest,
> Reflect the starry night upon its breast,
> So minds' by life's increasing tumult tossed,
> At death, may find the calm, in life, they lost.
>
> As windows, that no light can reach by day,
> At eve reflect the sun's departing ray;
> So souls, whom life's illusions rendered dark,
> As death draws near, receive Faith's Heavenly spark;
> The choice when narrowed, leaves the way more clear,
> And loss of earth, to them draws Heav'n more near.

8

The Woodpecker Art Club

Mary Fitch was born with a silver spoon in her mouth. She was the only daughter of Robert Fitch, a self-made man, a chemist, antiquarian, collector, property magnate and local politician, who made sure that, even before his death, his daughter was an extremely wealthy woman. In 1882 she married George Radford Pym from Belper, a handsome, rather rakish looking man many years her junior and from a much less wealthy background, in a glamorous wedding at St Peter Mancroft in Norwich. The couple honeymooned in Paris — but the marriage was a mistake and they separated after just a few months. Mary came back to Norwich with only a new name to remind her of her husband, and moved into one of her father's houses, 10 Chapel Field. In 1893 she bought a house nearby called St Mary's Croft where she lived in considerable style with a young lady companion/housekeeper, Lilly Bull. Lilly was just 16 when she went to work for Mrs Pym and she was clearly overwhelmed to be treated almost as an equal — and by the stream of local celebrities that poured through Mrs Pym's drawing room. Many years later Lilly wrote a memoir about her time with Mrs Pym. She was

60. Lilly Bull as a young woman, arranging flowers for Mrs Radford Pym.

writing long after the events she was describing took place and she is somewhat shaky on dates and facts — but nonetheless it is a wonderful document, full of gossip and anecdotes, press cuttings and photographs, and it is on this memoir[1] that most of this chapter is based.

Mary Pym comes across as a determined, hospitable, eccentric little woman with an unfashionably ruddy complexion which she habitually disguised by wearing a fine blue veil. She was also a keen tricyclist, riding the 27 miles from Norwich to her house in Sheringham each summer, even when she was over 70, dressed in a too-short blue dress and large, stout, sensible boots. Victorian society was intolerant of oddity — but money talks. Mary Pym was interested in people and she knew everyone who was anyone in Norfolk society — and quite a lot of people that most of Norfolk society would have dismissed as being of no importance at all.

She was a philanthropist. In 1904 she donated three acres of her estate, the Woodlands

61. Mrs Radford Pym (left) at Sheringham, c.1918–20. It comes from Lilly Bull's Memoir and is entitled 'Taken Unawares'. Mrs Pym hated being photographed and she always wore a veil.

62. Mrs Radford Pym (second left) and a group of cyclists in 1902.

63. *Postcard of Sheringham, showing the clock tower that Mrs Radford Pym presented to the town.*

Plantation off Earlham Road, to the city to use as a park, she donated money to build the clock tower which stands in the centre of Sheringham and a house in Sheringham for the town to use as accommodation for the district nurse. She also left over £3,000 to the Norfolk and Norwich Hospital with which they bought Pym House to use as a nurses' home. Her father had donated his collection to the museum, Mary bequeathed furniture to Strangers' Hall.

She was also extraordinarily generous to her many friends and acquaintances when she thought they needed help. For example, when the theatre director, Nugent Monck, arrived in Norwich in 1909 he was introduced to Mrs Pym and in conversation he expressed an interest in the old houses of Norwich. She suggested that he might be interested to see round a house that she owned – the Crypt in Ninham's Court. He was so delighted with it that she rented it to him at 6s a week for life then left it to him in her will.[2] When another friend, James Hooper the antiquarian, a convivial man much given to drink, died leaving his widow virtually penniless, Mrs Pym and several friends clubbed together to support the unfortunate Mrs Hooper and get her 'elected' to a vacancy at Cooke's Hospital.

According to Lilly Bull, Kate Nichols was Mary's 'greatest friend'. Lilly described her as 'that wonderful personality and woman of genius' and was sure that 'It was the peculiarity of her temperament that made Miss Nichols such a charming person to know and kept her surrounded by a host of devotees. She was a woman of restless, questing mind, amazingly rapid in speech, talking of all things but never talking nonsense . . . a lover of all that was beautiful. She had a range of information that seemed to embrace most things worthy of a human creature's thought and breath, more especially religion, philosophy and art.'³ Lilly was certainly spellbound by Kate's stories of her adventures in France and Cornwall and repeated many of them verbatim. Kate Nichols and Mary Pym were both unusual women and they were both on their own; it is quite possible that they had known each other since they were girls for their fathers were both on the City Council. By 1889, Kate was firmly established as a member of Norwich's Roman Catholic community and there appeared to be no likelihood that the rift with her family would ever be healed, she was living in lodgings away from the family home, her accommodation cannot have been what she was used to and perhaps she was depressed. Mary Pym herself was a devout Anglican, but she was open-minded about religion and had never allowed Kate's conversion to interfere with their friendship. In 1889 she decided to plan a little — actually quite a big — surprise to cheer her friend up, and also to indulge her own interest in the arts. The original idea seems to have come from another friend, Miller Smith, a (relatively) well-known artist and engraver who taught at the School of Art.

One evening Mrs Pym invited her friend to an event in Prince of Wales Road. When Kate arrived there were a handful of local artists there, five men and one lady — probably people she already knew though Lilly Bull does not tell us their names. Miller Smith was there too, along with Mary Pym. There was a small stage at the end of the room and steps up to it, all covered in red cloth, and on the stage was an arch of flowers and a high-backed chair covered in draperies and more flowers. Kate was welcomed warmly and, with much pomp and ceremony was asked to mount the stage and take a seat on the improvised throne. She was then invited to become president of a new club, to be named the Woodpecker Art Club, and when she agreed — she was probably too bemused to do anything else — they crowned her with a wreath of leaves and presented her with a sceptre! Miller Smith had devised the club's name — 'woodpecker' — because he, and several of the other founder members, were wood engravers, and wood engravers and carvers were often known as woodpeckers. Kate was, of course, an etcher, working on metal — but that did not seem to be a consideration. Lilly cannot have been at the ceremony herself as it took place some four years before she went to work for Mrs Pym, but she had obviously heard the story many times.

Kate would remain president of the Woodpecker Art Club until her death 34 years later, and she became so firmly associated with the club that some accounts describe her as its founder. Mrs Pym was also deeply involved and remained a committee member all her life, and she was almost certainly instrumental in signing up the other influential people who became Vice-presidents and committee members.

Lilly lists various Vice-presidents but they changed over time and some of the

Founded 1887.

NORWICH.

THE WOODPECKER ART CLUB.

President :

MISS C. M. NICHOLS, R.E., S.M.

Vice-Presidents :

THE HONOURABLE SYBIL AMHERST.

THE RIGHT HONOURABLE AUGUSTINE BIRRELL,
P.C., K.C., L.L.D.

SIR T. DIGBY PIGOTT, C.B., J.P.

WALTER RYE, ESQ.

W. NUGENT MONCK, ESQ.

H. COOPER PATTIN, ESQ., M.A., M.D. (Cantab.)

Committee :

MRS. G. RADFORD PYM.

MRS. CYRIL FITT.

MISS BURGESS.

MR. PERCY BROOKS.

MR. ARTHUR E. JACKSON *(Hon. Sec.)*

64. Brochure for the Woodpecker Art Club, date unknown.

ones on Lilly's list did not come to Norfolk until the early years of the twentieth century so they cannot have been there from the start. It sounds as if they were really trustees, there to add lustre to the club's brochure, rather than active participants. They included the Honourable Sybil Amherst, the Right Honourable Augustine Birrell PC, KC, LLD, Sir Thomas Digby Piggott, CB, JP and H. Cooper Pattin, MA, MD. Sybil Amherst was one of the Amhersts of Didlington, a family of blue stocking sisters whose father collected antiquities and financed Howard Carter's expeditions to Egypt; Mary Pym was friendly with all the Amhersts but Sybil was her particular favourite. Augustine Birrell was a barrister, writer and politician and became Chief Secretary for Ireland in 1907. He resigned in the wake of the Easter Rising in 1916. He lived in London, but no doubt Mrs Pym knew him because he had a house in Sheringham where she owned several properties and spent a good part of each summer. Sir Thomas Digby Piggott was another of her Sheringham contacts. He was a member of the Upcher family, a writer and natural historian who 'had a career of great usefulness in official life' — at least according to Lilly. H. Cooper Pattin was the first full-time medical officer of health for Norwich. Sometime after 1900 they were joined by Walter Rye and Nugent Monck. Walter Rye was a well-known Norwich antiquarian and genealogist, a keen athlete, a former London lawyer and something of an eccentric. (During his mayoral year he had to entertain Edward VII when the king visited Norwich; Mr Rye declined to dress in a frock coat for the occasion but insisted on wearing his everyday Norfolk jacket and pork pie hat.) Nugent Monck was an actor and theatre director who settled in Norwich before the First World War and founded the Maddermarket Theatre in what had been the Chapel of St John Maddermarket where Kate was baptised. One wonders how she viewed the transformation. Later their number would be swelled by Professor George Walter Baynham, an authority on Shakespeare, and Prince Frederick Duleep Singh. How seriously these busy people took their duties as Vice-presidents of the Woodpecker Club is open to question.

The committee members were Mrs Pym, Mrs Cyril Fitt, Miss Burgess and Mr Percy Brooks. They were later joined by Mr Arthur Jackson who was the club secretary for over 20 years. Mrs Cyril Fitt was a fine water colourist, working under her maiden name, Gertrude Howes. Of Miss Burgess and Percy Brooks we know very little. 'Miss Burgess' may well have been Rosetta Burgess who was an art teacher in Great Yarmouth, Percy Brooks was a merchant and Arthur Jackson an accountant — and eventually he married Lilly Bull.

The club had certain rules,[4] designed to set standards and — no doubt — to keep out undesirables. The annual subscription was 10s 6d, and though there was a literary branch of the society over which Walter Rye presided, the majority of the club members were to be artists or art lovers. Literary members paid an additional subscription of 5s 6d a year. They originally met at the School of Music in Rampant Horse Street, but over the years they had many venues. For each meeting their room was hung with brown holland (coarse linen) — a neutral background which was thought to be a suitable backdrop for paintings as it did not distract the eye — and members' work was laid out on shelves for all to see, admire and criticise.

There was no fixed schedule; meetings were held periodically for 'friendly, artistic and literary intercourse' and at each one a member or guest would present a short paper — and the lady members took it in turn to provide tea and cakes. 'Our evenings', wrote a former member, 'were delightful, friendly and unconventional.'[5] The lectures were an eclectic mix of whatever happened to interest one of the more vocal members at any given time — 'The Mediaeval Rood Screen', 'Norwich Silk Weavers', 'War Songs' and 'Ignorance in Action' were typical of the range of subjects on offer.[6] Lilly Bull's future husband was in charge of arranging the lectures and she gives us a good deal of detail about the ones she found memorable. She particularly enjoyed those given by Walter Rye on a variety of topics because it seems he was something of a comedian — there was one on the 'Street Nuisances' which beset the hapless pedestrian and apparently his pet hates were children's go-carts and babies' prams. He gave one talk that described in humorous detail the progress of an airship over Norwich in 1917, another was about practical jokes and yet another was entitled 'Retort and Repartee'. Various members — including Kate — joined in with examples. Canon Marcon, the Rector of Edgefield, lectured on 'Norfolk Words and Phrases'; Lilly was impressed that the examples he cited were drawn from real life rather than from books — which perhaps gives an idea of the quality of some of the other offerings. Professor George William Baynham often lectured about Shakespeare and Dickens and in 1921 Prince Frederick Duleep Singh presented 'A Few Notes on some of the Lesser Known East Anglian Painters' at the Maddermarket Theatre. He had spent a good deal of time scouring local sale rooms and country houses and had amassed quite a collection of works, some of which were exhibited to accompany the lecture. Kate Nichols took copious, though not very informative, notes and preserved them carefully — they are now in the Norfolk Record Office.[7]

The Prince was something of a catch. His father had fled to England from the Punjab as a 10-year-old boy in 1849 after the second Sikh War, and was given a pension by the British government in recognition of his family's support of Britain. The young boy was much feted — apparently he was a particular favourite of Queen Victoria — and lived in luxury at Elveden in Suffolk. But in the 1880s, for reasons that remain unclear, he persuaded himself that if he allied himself with tsarist Russia and turned his back on his former protectors he would get his kingdom back. The whole affair reads like a spy story — the Prince got entangled with Irish revolutionaries, Russian nationalists and Islamic seers, he spent months in Paris and visited Moscow — all the time with the British secret service keeping a close eye on his movements. It was a predictable disaster and Duleep Singh ended his days penniless and disgraced.[8] Frederick Duleep Singh was his son by his first wife, the Maharani Bamba, and had grown up as an East Anglian country gentleman, who, despite his exotic name and appearance, was far more interested in art and history than in the politics of his father's birthplace. He lived in Thetford at Blo Norton Hall. Nonetheless, he was a prince, and as such was to be courted — Mrs Pym invited a carefully selected band of friends to tea to meet him before the lecture.

From the first it was decided that the club would hold an annual exhibition of members' work — and it was written into the rules that no item was to be priced at less than a guinea! In time there were more and more social activities — boating on the Broads, trips to places of interest, an annual summer excursion to Sheringham to be entertained at Mrs Pym's cottage, even amateur dramatics at Christmas. Another of Mrs Pym's useful contacts was Mrs Margaret Pillow who, after her husband died in 1910, ran a high-class confectionery business called 'Princes' in Castle Street. The Woodpecker Club held an annual 'conversazione' there in a suite of rooms upstairs that was made available to them for the evening. Mrs Pillow wrote books on domestic economy and was the widow of a senior figure in the County Council Education Department. She was an enthusiastic member of the club and had enrolled both her sons as members as soon as they were born.

The 'Woodpeckers' were a motley crew, a mixture of professionals and semi-professionals, amateurs and eccentrics. Alfred Munnings was probably the club's most famous member, then an uncouth young man with an unusual taste in dress. Lily Freeman, one of the Norwich School of Art's star pupils, was an early member, as was the artist Ernest Sawford-Dye. He held a drawing class for the Woodpeckers and for a time had 77 students — which gives some idea of how large the club must have been in its early days. Ernest emigrated to Canada in 1903.[9] Berthalina Mann was a member in the early 1900s. She was a talented artist who had studied in London and sold work through Jarrolds and took commissions from Raphael Tuck — and she was less than impressed by her fellow members. 'They are certainly the queerest lot of people,' she confided to her diary in August 1910, describing an outing to Sheringham. The whole party had been invited to tea by Mrs Pym and she met them at the station dressed in the outfit she often wore at the seaside 'a sky-blue cotton dress and a blue gauze veil on her funny, mahogany-coloured old face'. Bertie was a rather unpleasant young woman and seldom had a good word to say about anyone; she went on to mock the afternoon's entertainment. 'We squashed into her tiny sitting room to eat bread and butter, ham sandwiches, jelly, tipsy cake and meringues' and to meet Alastor 'the seer (I feel sure he would approve entirely this description of himself) . . .'[10]

The club was an important part of Kate's life — her last public outing was in October 1922, three months before she died, to hear Augustine Birrell talk to club members at the Maddermarket Theatre. Sadly, most of the club's papers have been lost so we have no clear idea of the membership, or the programme, or who was on the committee when. On Kate's death in January 1923, Frederick Duleep Singh took over as president, but he, like Mrs Pym and many of the other club members, was growing old. He died in 1926. Nugent Monck was the third and final president, but by then the club was running out of steam. Mary Pym had been its guiding light and she died in the spring of 1927. Arthur Jackson had supported her for many years, but on her death he resigned as secretary and married Lilly Bull. They moved to Sheringham to St Luke's Cottage which Mrs Pym had left them in her will.

65. Lilly and Arthur Jackson in Sheringham in the 1930s.

However, Mrs Pym did live long enough to ensure that the Woodpeckers honoured Catherine Nichols appropriately. She arranged for the painting that Edward Elliot had done of Kate 20 years previously to be purchased and donated to the Castle Museum. Lilly Bull wrote loyally that the portrait was an exceptionally good likeness, though more discerning viewers might find the proportion and position of Kate's arms in their enormous leg o' mutton sleeves somewhat curious. Prince Duleep Singh presided over the ceremony and gave a speech at which he claimed Kate was too well known 'both socially and artistically' to require description — in fact he had not really known her well at all so it may have been a convenient get out. Some of Kate's friends from the Woodpecker Committee attended — Mrs Cyril Fitt and Miss Burgess who had been there from the beginning; Arthur Jackson, the long-standing secretary; and two later members, Horace Tuck, Vice-president of the Norwich School of Art and Lawrence Linnell, the Birmingham artist. Sybil Amherst sent her apologies as did Kate's brother Frederick, but her brother Alfred was there along with two of her Banister cousins, her old school friend Mary Mann (Polly Rackham) and her husband, Fairman, and a long list of other acquaintances.

In 1927 the Woodpecker Art Club merged with the Norwich Art Circle. The two organisations were similar, as we shall see, and the membership overlapped — Kate herself had been a member of the Art Circle since its foundation in 1885 —

so the idea of merging the two societies was an obvious one and had in fact been mooted as early as 1925. But the disappearance of the Woodpecker Club signalled the end of a typically Victorian venture which Kate Nichols had successfully steered for over 30 years. It survived her by just five.

66. Portrait of Catherine Maude Nichols, c.1895, by Edward Elliot,
presented to Norwich Castle Museum in her memory in 1923.

9

'Conversazioni of an Art character'

The Norwich Art Circle was founded in 1885, and was the brainchild of Charles John Watson, Kate's friend and neighbour, Edward Elliot, who would later paint the portrait of her that is in Norwich Castle Museum, and Robert Bagge Scott. All three were prominent members of the art scene in late nineteenth-century Norwich. Charles Watson was the first president of the Circle, Edward Elliot took over the presidency in 1887 when Watson married and moved to London, and Robert Bagge Scott became president some years later. It was agreed that the society would hold at least one exhibition a year and the annual subscription would be one guinea. The 'Rules' (included in the first catalogue) stated 'That the objects of the Norwich Art Circle be to bring together Artists, Amateurs and others interested in Art, to provide periodicals, books and catalogues, having reference to Art, to arrange for the exhibition in the Society's Room, or elsewhere, of Pictures, Drawings and other works of Art, to render the Society a centre where conversazioni may be held of an Art character, and generally to promote a knowledge and love of the Fine Arts.'

Kate joined the Circle as soon as it was formed. The Woodpecker Club was by then seven years old and quite well established but, like Kate, many of its members seem to have welcomed the opportunity to exhibit elsewhere as well.

There were 46 members of the Circle at the time of the first exhibition in 1885, but only 14 were exhibitors. As with the Woodpecker Club, many members were simply people interested in art, who enjoyed going to exhibitions and meeting artists but who were not themselves painters or sculptors or engravers. They included local worthies like R. J. Colman, the Bolingbrokes, B. W. Harcourt and S. J. J. Jarrold — and Alfred Barnard, son of a local ironmonger and the disappointed suitor of Kate's close friend, Mary Mann, née Polly Rackham. Polly's solicitor brother, William Simon, would later become a member too. In the early days nearly all the members lived in Norwich or Norfolk, but within quite a short time, artists in London and elsewhere were sending work to the exhibitions, though admittedly most of them were people with Norfolk connections. At its height the Circle had upwards of 80 members.[1]

Charles Watson and his friends were ambitious. They originally planned to hold three exhibitions a year — a 'black-and-white' exhibition in the spring, a summer retrospective exhibition of the work of one of Norwich's famous artists, and an autumn exhibition of members' work in a range of media. From the start, the society had its own premises in the Old Bank of England Chambers on Queen Street and they employed a caretaker to ensure the rooms were kept in good order and were open to members whenever they were needed. There were social get-togethers every Monday, informal weekly sketching meetings on Wednesdays and occasional classes, workshops and lectures on topics of interest — print-making classes were particularly popular. We do not know how many of these activities Kate attended but she certainly exhibited regularly at both the spring and autumn exhibitions. The Circle produced catalogues of each exhibition — Norfolk Record Office has a complete run of the ones from 1885 to 1900. They are beautifully printed on handmade paper and illustrated with a selection of engravings of exhibitors' work. Unfortunately the quality of the catalogues declined after 1900; they were produced in a smaller format on cheaper paper and the beautifully engraved illustrations were replaced by grainy photographs.

The Circle had to tailor its ambitions in other ways too. They soon outgrew the premises in Queen Street, and in 1899 the September exhibition was held in Bank Plain Assembly Rooms. After that they used St Peter's Hall and in 1907/08 the society gave up its rooms in the Bank of England Chambers completely as they were proving too expensive to maintain.

We also know that the plan for retrospective exhibitions did not last long: there was a show of paintings by John Thirtle (1777–1839) in July 1886, one of work by James Stark (1794–1859) in the summer of 1887 and, most important of all, a huge display of the work of John Sell Cotman (1782–1842) in July 1888. The illustrated catalogue of the Cotman exhibition was the largest the Circle ever produced and remains an important reference work for students. It is hard to know how popular these exhibitions were, but we do know that Kate Nichols was one of just 19 people

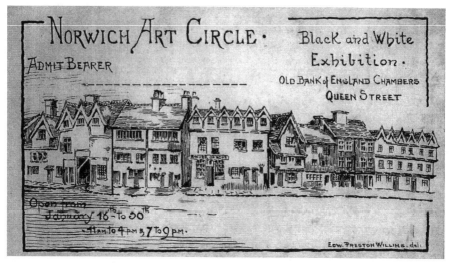

67. *Invitation to a Norwich Art Circle Exhibition, date unknown.*

listed as attending the private view of the Cotman show. Perhaps because of the amount of work and cost involved in that exhibition there was no retrospective in the summer of 1889, but the Circle put on an extra show of members' work in the July. There would be just one more retrospective, in 1891, of work by Edward Thomas Daniell (1804–42). However, the Circle did not give up on the idea entirely and though there were no more summer exhibitions, the May exhibition of 1905 included a handful of works by Frederick Sandys, shown alongside the engravings and black and white drawings of the members. The following year featured work by Henry Ninham – Kate must have been pleased to exhibit alongside one of the artists whose work was so like her own. There was a pause for a few years and then in 1913 the Circle was offered a loan collection of drawings by several members of the Norwich School – Crome, Cotman, Bright, Thirtle, Kitton, Ladbrooke and M. E. Cotman – which they gratefully accepted as a way of 'bulking out' the Black and White exhibition. By 1913 the number of members working in black and white had declined to the point where the exhibitions were barely viable. They were discontinued in 1914, ostensibly on account of the war.

Kate was always a mainstay of the Black and White exhibitions but she also contributed oils, watercolours or etchings to almost all of the autumn shows. She was the third largest contributor to the first exhibition in 1885, showing five works, including two of Lourdes which she had recently visited. Charles Watson exhibited eleven works and J. Miller Marshall showed eight, but most of the other eleven exhibitors contributed just one or two items. The critic at the *Eastern Daily Press* was not impressed. The *Norwich Argus* of 15th September was less critical of the exhibition as a whole but singled out one of Kate's works for particular criticism:

> Miss Nichols is well to the front with several strong bits of the dingy delight in watercolour which we expect of her. In all her efforts she is successful — in all, we might say, but 'Lourdes' which most people will be inclined to view as a hard, if not hideous smudge. In 'My Attic' (a), 'La Paroisse, Lourdes' (29), 'Vespers' (31) and 'Reeds' (35) she does herself every justice, the last named being a particularly powerful picture of night and nature.

Kate showed a number of French subjects again at the 1886 exhibitions, pictures of Lourdes and nearby Betharram in the Hautes Pyrenees alongside a dry-point of Normandy that she had already shown at the Royal Academy in 1877. As a recent convert it is quite likely that she would have made a trip to Lourdes and to the grottos and shrines at Betharram in the early or mid-1880s. She also exhibited views of Kynance in Cornwall, though these again may have been earlier works. However, the engraving of hers that the committee chose to illustrate in the catalogue of the 1886 black and white exhibition was a Norwich subject, 'Widdow's Ferry' (see plate 69).

The September 1886 catalogue was the first to contain prices, and Kate's pictures were comparatively cheap at between two and six guineas apiece — especially given that one of Robert Bagge Scott's works was offered at £55 and one of Edward Elliot's at £84. In 1887 Kate priced one of her oils, 'On Norwich River', at ten guineas. That work is now in the Castle Museum and is now entitled 'Riverside, Norwich' (see plate 30). She seldom charged more than ten guineas for her oil paintings, although in 1888 she was asking fifteen guineas for 'Woodland scene' and in 1898 she offered a painting entitled 'Evening' for a whopping, and wholly exceptional, £52 10s. With the inflation that followed the First World War, prices rose and Kate then regularly asked £21 and more for her larger oil paintings and her watercolour prices rose too to between six and eight guineas. Prints were still comparatively cheap at two to four pounds.[2]

We can also see that she offered the same subjects — and had them accepted — for exhibition more than once, which seems to show rather poor judgement on the part of the Hanging Committee. Indeed, the *Eastern Daily Press* was often quite critical of Art Circle exhibitions and frequently commented that the Committee was not sufficiently selective in the choice of work. On 6th October 1896, for example, their art critic was exceptionally scathing: 'there were pictures (which may be identified without the slightest assistance) that ought never to have been sent to any exhibition. . . . There is all the difference in the world between assuming an unreasonably exclusive attitude and finding a place in the Society's Gallery for any ill-conceived and ill-considered trifle.'

It was not the only time the local critics had attacked the Art Circle. On 17th October 1891 there was a particularly unpleasant review of the 18th Art Circle exhibition in the *Eastern Daily Press* which accused Catherine Nichols and a fellow artist, Mr Browne, of not taking their work seriously enough.

> *During the last few years, two phases of art have largely influenced English students. We refer to the French school and the Impressionist movement. . . . It is in the latter [i.e. the room devoted to oil paintings] that the fascination of Impressionism shows its influence on local artists. Here are a number of works by Miss C. M. Nichols and Mr H. E. J. Browne which convey the idea that these artists are inclined to coquet with art rather than take her seriously. A large number of the exhibits are so [sic] subjects and Miss Nichols contributes eight of them. Useful and interesting, doubtless, as notes of colour and effect, a studio portfolio would be a more appropriate place for them than the walls of a gallery. Such titles as 'The Muse of the Shore' (71) and 'The Sweep of the Tide' may be pretty, but this lady can hardly expect us to look on the canvases they indicate as being representative of her, or suitable for a public exhibition. In No 97 'At Sea' there is a boat that is distinctly bad in drawing and gives the impression of being built of paper. Miss Nichols is capable of doing good work, which makes the sending of such things hardly fair to herself, or to the Art Circle. If such a society is to be useful and retain its reputation, it is surely the duty of members to contribute nothing but sterling work to its exhibitions, or work at least that shows earnestness of purpose.*

Not surprisingly, Kate was furious and on 23rd October the paper published a long letter from her. It began: 'My principle [sic] objective in writing this is to protest against the style of witticism adopted by the person who wrote the Art Circle notice in your columns last Saturday.' She was careful not to appear to take umbrage at the criticism of her own works but instead affected to be offended on behalf of Mr Browne — 'such sneering remarks as "but why cotton wool instead of foam?" do not impress us artists with a high opinion of your critic's capability.' As to the criticism of her choice of subject matter, she replied that she was in good company — Turner, Henry Moore and Whistler had all painted similar subjects and she was happy to be bracketed with them. She was also pleased the critic thought her capable of good work and pointed out that, if he had taken the trouble to look, he would have found many London critics agreed with him!

68. 'At sea' by Catherine Maude Nichols, exhibited in the Norwich Art Circle Autumn exhibition of 1891. Lithograph. The Eastern Daily Press critic considered the boat to be extremely badly drawn!

However, she thought the real reason for his snide remarks was that he didn't like English artists to go abroad. She claimed that it was the unimaginative teaching in many art schools that drove artists to seek inspiration elsewhere. 'The truth is, your critic lets it escape that he is piqued at English artists deserting England for more congenial soil. France is the home of the artist: England has driven away her sons to Paris and Antwerp by her evident incapacity for teaching.' She was also nettled by his comments on her drawing of the boat in 'At sea' — 'I have probably drawn more boats on copper than your critic has on paper, and though I don't profess infallibility I question whether my boat can be proved to be very much out,' she wrote defensively. There was a good deal more of the same, then she went on: 'Why should the careful work of an observant eye be dismissed at the will of a captious being who has too little discernment to distinguish merit when not already notified to him?' And she ended by listing less well-known members of the group whose work she thought deserved mention alongside the better-known artists the critic had praised.

In the next issue of the paper the editor felt obliged to explain himself: 'It would be ungracious on our part,' he wrote, 'to engage a gentleman to write an article in our columns and allow it to be so seriously assailed by a correspondent without an explanation. The critic was recommended to us as well qualified to write an article, and we have every reason to believe that the article was a bona fide one. But who shall decide in matters of taste?'

However, adverse criticism never deterred Kate Nichols and as time went by the critics grew kinder. On 27th October the *Eastern Daily Press* commented that there 'is a good deal of elevated feeling in Miss C. M. Nichols' "Horning" (143), a quality all the more worthy of remark in that the artist has sought for no unusual atmospheric effects but has contented herself with recording the normal greyness of a Broadland sky and waterscape.' Kate herself had dismissed 'Horning' as a mere sketch. 'Feeling' was apparently important to the *Eastern Daily Press*. In May 1905 her rather pedestrian etching of a French chateau (see plate 26) was commended as treating the subject 'with perfect feeling'.

She continued to exhibit with the Art Circle at almost every exhibition; indeed her work often dominated the show. Most artists submitted two or three works, a few occasionally offered five or six — but year after year Kate displayed seven or more items, sometimes ten or a dozen. And in May 1912 Kate's work — fourteen items — made up almost a quarter of the black and white exhibition. Even in 1922, just months before her death, she submitted ten pieces, in a range of media, to that year's exhibition. She also seems to have been quite pernickety about how her work was presented. In the black and white exhibitions most artists were content simply to allow the audience to enjoy their pictures — Kate Nichols insisted on telling people how pieces were produced — 'drypoint', 'charcoal', 'lithograph', 'special proof', 'advance proof' and so on. She also made sure that if a work had been exhibited somewhere prestigious there was mention of it in the catalogue. Visitors to the black and white exhibition

69. Illustration of 'Widdow's Ferry' by Catherine Maude Nichols from the Norwich Art Circle catalogue for 1889. Dry-point. The image is actually dated 1885.

70. 'A sea piece' by Catherine Maude Nchols from the Norwich Art Circle exhibition 1889.
Lithograph.

in May 1910 were made aware that a version of 'Trowse Hythe' was 'now hung in the Public Library in New York'; in 1911 they were informed that a print of 'A bye street in Cornwall' that they were lucky enough to be viewing had been exhibited at the Paris Salon earlier in the year. It is unlikely that any of this endeared Kate Nichols to the other members of the Art Circle.

71. 'Old houses, Yarmouth' by Catherine Maude Nichols. Dry-point. From the catalogue of the Norwich Art Circle Black and White exhibition in 1903. Note the empty foreground so typical of her compositions.

72. 'Houses at Lakenham' by Catherine Maude Nichols. Dry-point. From an exhibition catalogue
of the Norwich Art Circle in 1904.

The following table of works she exhibited at Art Circle exhibitions between 1885 and 1900 may be of interest. The few exhibitions missing from the sequence are either the retrospectives of the Norwich School artists mentioned above, or ones to which Kate did not contribute.

Year	Exhibition	Number of CMN exhibits	Catherine Maude Nichols — works and titles (* denotes an illustration in the catalogue)
1885	1st	5	'My attic', 'La Paroisse, Lourdes', 'Vespers', 'Reeds', 'Lourdes'
1886	2nd (b&w)	11	'Norwich river', 'Betharram, Hautes Pyrenees', 'Crown Point', 'Rue des Cordonniers at Dives, Normandy', 'Late evening', 'Widdow's Ferry'*, 'Reeds', 'Lion Rock, Kynance Cove', 'Cow Hill', 'St John's, Cambridge', 'Une Méditation dans la Paroisse a Lourdes'
1886	4th	5	'Fort and town of Lourdes', 'Old Barge Yard, King Street', 'The cave, Lourdes', 'The Horse, Kynance', 'Notre Dame de Lourdes'
1887	5th (b&w)	6	'At Oulton Broad', 'At Lourdes', 'Windmill at Brundall', 'Betharram', 'Rue Basse, Lourdes', 'A corner'

1887	7th	4	'On Norwich river', 'East wind at Brundall', 'At Hoveton Broad', 'At Hoveton St John'
1888	8th (b&w)	6	'Fidelity', 'On the eastern coast', 'At Oulton Broad', 'A Cornish street', 'Per la Festa', 'Norfolk scene'
1888	10th	5	'Cloudy weather', 'Woodland scene', 'Summer sunlight', 'Trees and clouds', 'Trees at twilight'
1889	11th (b&w)	5	'Norfolk church', 'Dark Entry Lane', 'Street in Cornwall', 'Byeway on the coast'*, 'At Carrow'
1889	12th	11	'Exterior of Strangers' Hall', 'Dean's Meadow, the Close', 'Riverside, St Anne's Wharf', 'Widdow's Ferry', 'Cow Hill', 'Charing Cross', 'Old houses, Ber Street, now pulled down', 'Staircase, Strangers' Hall', 'Cloisters, Norwich Cathedral', 'Old court, Surrey Street', 'St Helen's cloisters'
1889	13th	6	'Floods at Thorpe', 'While misty vapours roll', 'Salt marshes', 'A bit of colour', 'At Salhouse', 'A sea piece'*
1890	14th (b&w)	6	'Wiveton church', 'A literary litter', 'Trees', 'Cley church', 'St Helen's cloisters', 'A landscape'
1890	15th	8	'Road to the sea', 'Westlegate Street, Norwich', 'Cley mill', 'A cloud effect', 'Brundall causeway', 'Cley bank at evening', 'Wiveton church', 'Wiveton stone bridge'
1891	16th (b&w)	3	'The village street' (2 versions), 'The road to the sea', 'A subject for reflection'
1891	18th	9	'A wave', 'A calm', 'The muse of the shore', 'Sea study', 'Up our court', 'The sweep of the tide', 'Sea study', 'Flood tide', 'At sea'
1893	21st (b&w)	2	'The manor', 'A rainy day'
1893	22nd	2	'From my staircase', 'At Reedham'
1894	23rd (b&w)	1	'At Golders Hill'

1895	25th (b&w)	1	'Wind'
1896	28th	2	'Twilight', 'In the garden'
1897	29th (b&w)	2	'Looking west', 'In north Norfolk'
1897	30th	6	'Waste ground', 'Brundall', 'Vista from a window in Surrey Street', 'Hautbois church', 'Salhouse Broad', 'Woodland scene'
1898	31st (b&w)	2	'On Wroxham Broad', 'A quiet scene'
1898	32nd	7	'Mousehold', 'Lone farm', 'In March', 'In a garden', 'Evening', 'A verandah scene', 'Rushes'
1899	33rd (b&w)	6	'Bare branches', 'Winter'*, 'Afterglow', 'Alders', 'Elms', 'Windswept'
1899	34th	3	'Erpingham Gate', 'Catton', 'Wroxham'
1900	35th (b&w)	3	'Wind and water', 'Somerleyton'*, 'Catton'*, 'Cley church'
1901	37th (b&w)	9+	'Trees in March', 'After Edward Elliot', 'Whitlingham', 'Ipswich Road', 'Branches', 'Pencil drawings', 'Wroxham', 'Marshland', 'The haunted pool'
1901	38th	1	'Brancaster'* (oil)
1902	39th (b&w)	3	'Brancaster Staithe'*, 'Passing shadow', 'May evening, Ipswich Road'
1902	40th	7	'Miss Brae', 'Miss Valéry Hornor, daughter of Francis Hornor, Esq', 'Miss Marjery Nichols, daughter of Lt Col F P Nichols RAMC' (miniatures); 'At the Kings Head', 'A city road', 'Horning, a sketch', 'Weather or no' (oils)
1903	41st (b&w)	6	'At Mousehold', 'Old houses, Yarmouth'*, 'Old pump, Thorpe', 'A dreadful place', 'Pointe de Bretagne', 'At twilight'
1903	42nd	2	'Old inn, Lakenham'*, 'The first gleam' (oils)
1904	43rd (b&w)	3	'Old houses, Lakenham'*, 'Lansdown Passage', 'Yarmouth'

1904	44th	4	'Spring foliage', 'A wooded path', 'Many leaves', 'A Norfolk dyke near Aylsham' (w/cols)
1905	45th (b&w)	2	'A French chateau', 'Cringleford'
1905	46th	2	'The bridge, Lenwade', 'The ford, Lenwade' (oils)
1906	47th (b&w)	5	'Charing Cross, Norwich' (litho), 'Lenwade ford', 'Lenwade Bridge Inn', 'Town trees', 'Storm effect, Brundall' (charcoal)
1906	48th	10	'A Calm, Sheringham', 'Sheringham looking east', 'Beeston Abbey', 'Old Sheringham', 'Attleborough Hall', 'Rough weather, Sheringham' (w/cols); 'G Watkins', 'Graves' (miniatures); 'Mousehold' (oils)
1907	49th (b&w)	5	'Elm Hill', 'The musicians', 'Grove Road, Norwich', 'Marine Cross, Norwich', 'Watchers'
1907	50th	6	'Old houses, Sheringham', 'Cringleford Mill', 'Low tide, Sheringham' (w/cols), 'Cringleford', 'Study of oak', 'Wroxham' (oils)
1908	51st (b&w)	6	'Guildhall, Norwich', 'Old Town, Lakenham', 'Norwich Castle', 'Beeston', 'Where wreathing vapours clothe the frowning craggs', 'Wind, grass and trees'
1908	52nd	6	'A portrait', 'Conflicting light', 'Bright Broadlands', 'Shadows', 'Dazzle', 'Quack, quack, quack'
1909	53rd (b&w)	9	'The late W. P. Nichols', 'Witches Row', 'The late Lord Leicester', 'The lone mill', 'High ground', 'Virgin's tomb', 'The Very Rev Canon Duckett', 'A quiet pool', 'Where fretted sunbeams thread the leafy shade'
1909	54th	7	'Buxton Lamas' (w/cols), '16th century house, Bignold's Court, Surrey St', 'Bignold's Court, Surrey St', 'The escape', 'A sketch', 'Near the Lizard', 'Cringleford' (oils)

1910	55th (b&w)	13	'Trowse Hythe', 'Rue des Cordonniers, Dives', 'Britons' Arms, Elm Hill', 'Sunlight, Somerleyton', 'Norwich Castle', 'St John the Baptist Catholic Church', 'Chips', 'Light and Shade', 'Study in pencil', 'Cley Bridge', 'A snowy day', 'Ipswich Road', 'Old Sheringham'
1910	56th	7	'The Abbey Car Langley', 'On the roads, Acle' (w/cols); 'Jim' (miniature);'Some poplars', 'Some trees', 'A cripple', 'Acle' (oils)
1911	57th (b&w)	5	'Pump Tree, Thorpe', 'Gadshill', 'A bye street in Cornwall', 'Old Hampstead', 'Fire and water', 'Wellington Street, Norwich'
1911	58th	4	'A breath of spring' (w/col), 'Companions', 'Acle', 'At Hautbois'
1912	59th (b&w)	14	'A forge', 'Docks, Bristol', 'Acle Road', 'St Peter's Hospital, Bristol', 'Mary-le-Port Street, Bristol', 'Cantley, Norfolk', 'Reeds, Wroxham', 'Brewers' Arms, Bristol', 'Suspension Bridge, Bristol', 'Whitlingham', 'Evening, Acle', 'Acle', 'The savage rock that circling mists enfold' (charcoal), 'Limpenhoe, Cantley'
1912	60th	6	'Haut-Vois, a sketch'[sic], 'The crypt, Norwich', 'My garden', 'Riverside, Norwich', 'The Bethel Hospital, Norwich' (oils)
1913	61st (b&w)	12	'The Bethel Hospital, Norwich', 'Chantry Court', 'Mancroft Yard', 'Roadway, Cley', 'Oulton', 'Cley church', 'Windmill, Cley', 'St Stephen's Church', 'a. Sheringham b. Yarmouth', 'Jungle, Acle', 'Crown Court', 'St Julian's Church'
1913	62nd	7	'East Ilsley', 'Old Street, Bodmin', 'Fowey, Cornwall', 'The Downs, East Ilsley', 'Golf links, Bodmin', 'Ninham's Court, Norwich', 'Cantley'

1914	63rd	7	'Mousehold', 'At Trowse', 'Acle' (w/cols); 'A Norfolk homestead', 'Whitlingham', 'Cherry Tree Farm', 'Solitude' (oils)
1915	64th	6	'Forty steps', 'A dweller by the river' (w/cols); 'The refuge', 'Whitlingham', 'Full bloom', 'Mousehold' (oils)
1916	65th	5	'Carrow rose garden' (w/col); 'Spring, Whitlingham', 'Twilight, Brundall', 'Autumn, Whitlingham', 'An old world garden, Catton' (oils)
1917	66th	7	'The quarry', 'Streamlands', 'On the Thames', 'Mountlands, Taunton', 'Whitlingham', 'Waterloo Bridge' (oils)
1918	67th	11	'The Dingle, Norwich', 'Study of trees', 'Taunton trees', 'The Flats', 'Early in the year', 'Cross roads', 'Firs' (oils); 'Cley-next-the-Sea', 'Stuart's Court, Norwich', 'Rheims', 'The Old Manor, Stiffkey' (engravings)
1919	68th	8	'The lake in the forest', 'A crown of firs', 'Fir land', 'Summer' (oils); 'Au bord du Lac', 'Mousehold', 'Mrs Savile Fielding' (w/cols); 'A lonely path' (engraving)
1920	69th	7	'A portrait', 'Life's old cottage, battered and decayed . . .' (w/cols); 'Carrow', 'Whitlingham', 'April' (oils); 'A lonely path', 'Willowy meads' (engravings)
1921	70th	3	'The roll of the land', 'Where willows and rushes in harmony dwell', 'A placid pool' (oils)
1922	71st	10	3 miniatures of trees, 'Where lacey films the leafage dark o'erspread', 'A French Mairie' (w/cols); 'Tall trees, Bracondale', 'The way to the river', 'Whitlingham', 'Open country, Hautbois' (oils); 'Old houses, Bristol' (etching)

IO

'Poetic duplicates'

'Miss Nichols says she has scarcely ever painted a picture that had not its poetic duplicate in rhythm in her mind,' wrote the interviewer from *The Women's Penny Paper* in 1889.

Lines of Thought and Thought in Lines was published in 1892 and contained some of Kate's etchings and their 'poetic duplicates', but it was not her first foray into print. In 1885 she had published her polemic about Catholicism (discussed in more detail in Chapter 7), a surprisingly outspoken document for a convert, and a female one at that. A year later, in 1886, she produced something much lighter — *Old Norwich* (or *A Novel of Old Norwich*, depending on whether you take the title from the cover or the flyleaf). This was a novella, or a long short story, set in Norwich and illustrated with a series of Kate's own etchings of the city. The story is simple — a pretty young girl, Lil, is visited by her sailor cousin, Ben, who has been in love with her for most of his life. Lil is fond of her cousin but has no intention of marrying him for she is in love with a German music teacher, Herr Vogel, who sees his pupils in a room downstairs from the one in which Lil lodges. Herr Vogel is a violinist and passionate about his music; unfortunately, Lil cannot

73. Cover of Old Norwich. *The front page describes it as 'A Novel of Old Norwich'.*

stand the sound of the violin. Nonetheless she rejects Ben's advances. Herr Vogel goes back to Germany and she does not see him for many months. Then she hears that he has been in a railway accident and has injured his hand so badly that he may never be able to play his beloved violin again. Lil rushes to Germany to be with him, they declare their love for each other, and she realises that she could happily put up with the violin music if only he recovers.

It is a simple little story but it is well written and there are some amusing touches — the room of Lil's downstairs neighbour into which Ben blunders by mistake is 'utterly wanting in the elements of the picturesque' and her two fashionable bonnets 'displayed their unqualified ugliness on an adjacent chair'. Ben puffs cigarette smoke at the 'melancholy canary' and he uses contemporary slang, he talks of 'pistolling' a rival and accepts Lil's rejection with commendable equanimity — 'I won't be tragic over it,' he promises. There are hints that Lil is something of a feminist — 'she sometimes remarked that if you happened to be fair, with blue eyes, and were not as ugly as sin, the accusation of being less wise than other people was not unlikely to be brought against you.' But Kate Nichols could not leave religion alone for long. She has the two young people discuss belief — Lil believes in immortality but Ben dismisses it as 'unfashionable'. Lil berates him and finishes by saying 'great affection sometimes ends in cutting us off from all earthly happiness, but yet opens up unthought-of possibilities of

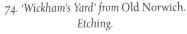

74. 'Wickham's Yard' from Old Norwich. Etching.

75. 'King Street' from Old Norwich. Etching.

happiness that do not altogether depend on this life'. It was a typical statement of Catherine Nichols' view of the world — though it does not sit well with the character she gives Lil.

Old Norwich was published by Jarrolds in a format that would become familiar in Kate's later work — the book was bound in a grey paper cover with one of Kate's etchings on the cover and the title in a rather strange script that she probably devised. The pages are of good quality paper and the edges — rather incongruously for such a slight volume — are gilt.

Jarrolds produced two more books for her the following year (1887) in a similar format. One was *Two Norfolk Idylls* and the other was *Musings at Cromer*. The two 'idylls' are again long short stories and are both heavily moralistic. The first is presented in the form of a story told by Aunt Sophia to her two young nieces and concerns her sister, their Aunt Lavinia. Both women are elderly spinsters, but in her youth Aunt Lavinia had had a boyfriend. She loved him and they got engaged but she treated him badly and flirted with other men. In despair he went off and joined the army. She thought that meant he no longer cared for her and was about to marry someone else — but as she stood at the altar the soldier

76. *Cover of* Two Norfolk Idylls.

returned, saw her with another man and left, heartbroken, without speaking to her. Stricken with remorse, she called the wedding off — but the soldier had not stayed long enough to know that. He believed she had married the other man and so went off to war — and, of course, he was killed.

Aunt Lavinia has a passion for lichens and spends a lot of time collecting them — it was a fashionable pastime for Victorian ladies — and a device, no doubt, that enabled Kate to include pictures of marshes and churchyards.

The second story is also about lost love. This time it concerns Madame Aline, a charming, wise old lady who was forbidden to marry her true love because he was French — this was during the Napoleonic wars. She never forgot him and never married anyone else — and one day she meets him again at a party. They

77. *'Costessey Hall' from Two Norfolk Idylls. Etching.*

78. *'Salhouse' from Two Norfolk Idylls. Etching.*

79. 'Trees' from Two Norfolk Idylls. *Etching.*

are old, it is too late for them to be happy together and within hours Madame Aline is dead — but not before having one last longing look at a set of topaz jewels he gave her when they were young lovers. She then makes a present of them to her great-niece who is about to marry one of the man's distant cousins.

The 'idylls' are competently written but there is no spark of humour, nothing to leaven the tragedies except the faint possibility that the younger generation will heed the example of their elders and lead happier lives. Kate's sister, Alice Powell, had given birth to a little girl in 1885 — were these stories of lost love intended for little Gwladys to read when she was older? Kate never mentions her family but that does not necessarily mean she had no contact with them.

The other book she produced in 1887 was a rather curious volume. *Musings at Cromer* was billed as a book to read on holiday, a souvenir of a visit to Cromer: 'the object of the present unpretending volume is to provide visitors to Cromer with a slight memento of various points of interest to be found in and near that picturesque little town, but also with a few ideas in prose and verse . . . [which] may lead the mind away from the visible beauty of the earth and sea to dwell on some of the graver thoughts suggested by that beauty.' It contains several of Kate's etchings of the town and the introductory essay extols the virtues of books over humans as holiday companions. 'How many annoying habits, too, are we not obliged to put up with if we conclude to take for our companion the average human being?' she wrote. It is hard to decide whether this was simply a justification for compiling the book in the first place, a tongue-in-cheek comment, or whether Kate Nichols herself did find other people's company tiresome when she was on holiday.

romer Sketches:

And Musings whilst there.

GM Nichols.S.S.GE.

Jarrold and Sons,
London and Norwich.

80. Cover of Cromer Sketches.

There are three more essays, all on serious subjects and all presenting Kate Nichols' view of the world. 'Modern materialism' begins with the confident assertion that 'Doubt as to the existence of a Creator may generally be traced to ignorance or a superficiality of thought,' and is a sermon on the existence of God. Kate expected her readers to agree with her — this was not an argument to convince the uncertain, it was to confirm the faith of the already devout. She was also keen to show her erudition, quoting Frederick the Great and Leibniz and the 'German scientists' who had produced evidence to discount 'cell theory' and to show the weaknesses of Darwinism. In 1887 Darwin's theories were still contentious and many saw them as a direct attack on religion — something Kate could never have countenanced. Instead she cited Reverend J. Cooke's *Monday Lectures*, a work now virtually unknown, which apparently proved 'that the soul is a force external to the nervous mechanism, and that the molecular motions of the particles of the latter are a closed circuit, not transmutable into the activities of the former'.

The next essay, 'Realization', is all about the love of God, the idea that everything that happens does so for a reason, and the importance of self-abnegation and submitting oneself to the God's will. 'Take a successful career, for instance,' wrote Kate, '— the proper label for that would be — a temptation to pride and self-indulgence.' Kate herself had a successful career and from the interviews she gave it would seem she was justifiably proud of her achievements; perhaps that sentence was a personal reminder for it is unlikely that many of her lady readers had careers of any sort, let alone successful ones. Again, the essay ends with a statement of faith: 'In the lucid words of the Catechism, we were made to know God, to love Him, and to serve Him in *this* world, and to be happy with Him for ever in the next.'

The third essay is a short one, entitled 'Platonics', and plays with the question of whether there is such a thing as platonic love. Kate decides there is, but that it is very rare.

The final entry is perhaps the most curious of all, and sits incongruously amongst the sermons and the moralising. It is a playlet entitled 'At Loggerheads. A Duologue'. Performing plays for family and friends was quite a popular activity for Victorian households and numerous short pieces were written for the purpose. This particular piece would have stretched the resources of most establishments, however, as it was set in the Australian outback and featured such everyday household objects as a tortoise with 'Norah' carved into its shell and a kitten with a wooden (why wood rather than leather?) collar similarly inscribed. The story concerns a young couple whose relationship is almost destroyed by misunderstandings. The connection to Cromer is tenuous to say the least — though at one point Norah does remind her boyfriend of how she 'made cigarettes' (presumably roll-ups) for him and a friend 'at Cromer'!

Interspersed with the essays is a series of poems of which 'The Dance of the Leaves' is far and away the most light hearted:

> In triplets and couplets they're footing it fast
> To the rise and the fall of the eddying blast,
> Bare branches above and a grey sky behind,
> See where the leaves dance, keeping time to the wind!
> List, list to the dance of the leaves.

But even that ends with intimations of the Creator:

> When rises the wind
> Then the dancers must dance.
> There are folks who say it's a game of mere chance
> That the wind blows the leaves, as the moon draws the sea.
> What makes the wind blow is the question for me.
> List, list to the dance of the leaves.

'Light and Love' is about lost love, but, as ever in Kate's writings, divine love triumphs over mere mortal affection.

> Light fades upon the western sea,
> Love melts away on shore,
> Faint light is left upon the sea,
> Faint love upon the shore.

One last bright beam a moment glows,
Love lasts almost as long —
The light has fled — the darkness grows,
Love's dead; but life is long.

And yet upon an eastern shore
Rose o'er life's storm-tossed waves,
A Love Divine, that evermore
Sheds light upon those waves.

The poem 'Friendship and Love' follows the essay about platonic love and arrives at the same conclusion which is that 'true friendship and true love' spring from the same source.

How differs friendship then from purest love?
It differs not in kind, but in degree:
Both to the earth descend from Heav'n above:
Both should from selfish hopes and aims stand free.

In 'Nature', the final poem in this volume, Kate describes the beauties of nature with an artist's eye for the changing colours of the sky.

Bounded by laws of harmony and change,
Degrees of beauty through all Nature range;
Where all is perfect, who can name the best,
The ocean calm — or, its sublime unrest?
Do gorgeous sunsets most delight our eyes,
Or calm unbroken [sic] of blue cloudless skies —
The gentle tints of lemon, pink and grey,
Pale messengers that usher in the day —
Or the majestic tones of gold and rose,
The courtiers rich that linger round its close?

Kate sometimes liked to play with words. An oil painting she submitted to the Art Circle exhibition in October 1902 was titled 'Weather or no' — 'a pictorial conundrum,' according to the *Daily Press* of 27th October, 'which is sufficiently determinable by reference to a louring sky above a damp and misty road'. Unfortunately, we do not know where the painting is now.

Kate's final book of poems also has a clever title — *Lines of Thought and Thought in Lines*. It was published in 1892 and is a more substantial work than any of her previous ones, and the poems are interspersed with her own etchings. A smaller, undated book containing seven of her poems also exists. It seems probable that this was produced some time between 1887 and 1892 (most of the poems it contains reappear in the later work) and perhaps it was sufficiently well-received for her to feel confident of producing a more extensive volume. Lines of Thought is dedicated to Lady Eastlake (1809–1893), a Norwich-born etcher, art critic, writer, regular contributor to *The Quarterly* art journal and the wife of Sir Charles Eastlake, Director of the National Gallery. She was born Elizabeth Rigby and did not marry until she was forty – it is quite possible that the Nichols and the Rigbys knew each other and that Kate and Elizabeth had met.

Lines of Thought seems to have been advertised and sold more widely than any of Kate's other books. On 2nd November 1892, for instance, the *Leeds Mercury* recommended this 'dainty book' to its readers. 'The writer is evidently a lover of nature and a student of mind and motive,' the critic wrote. 'A serious tone pervades nearly the whole of the poems' – and he went on to single out 'Illusions' and 'Dance of the Leaves' for special mention.

Some of the etchings in Lines of Thought relate to poems of the same name, like 'Rent Rocks' – 'Rent Rocks – where undisturbed the shadows lie' or 'Light at evening' – 'The golden river laps the shore/Where drowses an old city at its edge' but despite Kate's claim about poetic equivalence, the majority are not accompanied by illustrations. The poems are a mixed bag and the themes of lost love, earthly grief, God's omnipotence and love and the hope of happiness in the world to come recur time after time. In many of Kate's artworks the viewer

81. 'Rent rocks' from Lines of Thought and Thought in Lines.
Dry-point to accompany a poem with the same title.

82. *'Light at evening' from* Lines of Thought and Thought in Lines.
Dry-point to accompany a poem with the same title.

is led into the picture in the hope that there is something of real interest in the distance — round the corner, across the river, over the hill or through the trees. In her writings the reader is assured real happiness will only be achieved further on, in the world to come. Kate was a competent writer, she had an artist's eye, a grasp of language and the ability to use a range of different forms and metres, and for the most part she avoids banality and mawkish sentimentality, but the poems are nearly all fairly simplistic statements of Kate's unshakeable view of the world.

The titles alone give an idea of the content — 'Mortal Life', 'Peace at Death', 'Illusions', 'Life without Faith', 'The Mountain of Sin', 'The Realm of Perpetual Calm', 'Che Sara Sara', 'A Mock Heaven', 'The Traitor's Death' — Kate's unwavering faith and her passion for her religion come across loud and clear.

> *When o'er the verge of our dark planet's rim . . .*
> *With light divine and pure, so that the Birth*
> *Of Christ within it, kills all sin and strife*
> *Souls cast no shadows when they're wholly fused.*
>
> ('Sunrise')

> *At each sin we repent, there's a stone rolled away*
> *From the mountain of sin that has grown day by day . . .*
>
> ('Mountain of Sin')

> *Facts before they're believed must be known.*
> *There are those who in ignorance rest;*
> *The religion of Christ must be shown,*
> *By the many by whom 'tis professed,*

In their lives, 'ere its worth all will own,
And admit that its teachings are best.
                              ('Christmas')

When the leaves are thick and the flowers bloom
And the grass smells sweet in the ev'ning gloom . . .
There are some can see beyond nature's laws
Self-existing ever, The First Great Cause.
                    ('The Realm of Perpetual Calm')

Thus the bond of hope is the only tie
Betwixt those yet living, and those that die:
And for those who love, the sure place of tryst,
And the only one, is the Heart of Christ.
                                   ('Change')

As far as we know, Kate had a wide circle of friends and acquaintances and a deep and enduring friendship with Mrs Pym, yet many of her poems mourn the insubstantial nature of human relationships.

Then wherefore mourn the earth's fair show;
Lost friendship — shipwrecked love —
There is no friendship here below,
So true as that above.
                               ('Intangible')

Divided — How? — By words, a glance, a tear?
By creeping doubt, or mind not clearly read?
No matter how — Divided; once so near:
More parted now, than living are from dead.
Divided! Yes — the very word proclaims
The broken tie, that now no longer binds
The severed links, nor the far sundered aims.
Divided — once so near.
          ('The Friendship that can change was never true' St Jerome)

A number of the poems reflect Kate's love of nature, though she can seldom resist making some religious reference as well.

'Here's balm for your burning wound, my child!
Here's rosemary, rue, thyme and myrrh:
And the healing winds shall allay the pain:
And with joy shall Lethe's dark streams be fain,
All her innermost depths to stir:
That the coolest and clearest, most potent of waters,
May aid in restoring earth's fairest of daughters.'

The Reply
'The rosemary has no scent for me,
And the rue and the thyme no power:
The myrrh alone can for sin atone:
You may leave me this sweet flower.'
('Nature, Consolatrix: Loquatur')

Where no bird ever sings,
Where the white vapour clings
To the face of the black morass;

Where the green lizard glides
And the speckled toad hides
Neath the stones and the long damp grass;

Will I wait for my love,
Till the fireflies above
Shall gleam like the eyes of the lass.
('The Tryst')

A filmy web of gossamer,
Caught on a wild rose briar,
Transfixed by thorns, whilst threaded gems
Reflect the red sun's fire . . .
('Memory: Three Sketches. 1. Fancy')

Just occasionally Kate managed to write something lighter. We have already quoted 'Dance of the leaves' and she wrote another 'leafy' poem entitled 'From the leaves of the past to the leaves of today' from which we quote a couple of verses:

Well, time has convinced us we turn into coal;
And though you may think that's not much of a goal,
It proves we were made to form part of a whole,
And serve the one being on earth with a soul.

That being is man, who is matter and mind:
That we were his slaves he was not slow to find;
But, would you believe it, this man is so blind,
He swears he's all matter, and leaves out the mind!

Another poem that does not fit very closely with the religious gloom that pervades most of Kate's poetry is 'In Fairyland'. The first of its numerous verses runs:

In Fairyland I hold my court
Where blue-eyed flowers
At witching hours,
Reveal their powers
To sway my thought.

This was one of three of Kate's poems that were set to music by Claud H. Hill, a Norwich schoolmaster, and published as songs in the 1890s. The other two were 'Instead' and 'Dance of the Leaves'. Claud Hill (1870–1956) is best known for his 'Cycling Song' of 1897, but he wrote other pieces as well — 'Benedicite Omnia Opera No 2 in D' (1907), the 'Elise Gavotte' (1903), 'Three Pieces for Violin and Pianoforte' (1909) and set other people's work to music. We do not know whether Kate commissioned him to write the music or whether he volunteered his services, but the fact that she took the opportunity is yet another example of Kate's business sense and eye for ways of publicising her work.

The same year that *Lines of Thought* appeared Kate also published a very strange work, *Zoroaster, a Dramatic Fragment*. It is written in the form of a two-act play and is complete in itself, so it is hard to see why she chose to describe it as a 'fragment'. She claims in the introduction that it was inspired by a historical romance by Marion Crawford, and perhaps it appealed to her because it describes a tragic love affair. Francis Marion Crawford (1854–1909) was a prolific American author, noted for his weird and fantastical novels and short stories, many of which were set in Italy where he was born. His version of *Zoroaster* was published in 1885. The characters in Kate's play are Zoroaster, a magician, Nehushto, a Jewish princess, Darius, 'the great king' and Atossa, his queen. Nehushto loves Zoroaster but marries Darius (who is allowed four wives) because she believes

Zoroaster is in love with Atossa. This is a rumour spread by Queen Atossa herself because she is jealous of the beautiful young Nehushto. In the final scene it looks as if Zoroaster and Nehushto may finally be together — when a barbarian horde arrives at the temple at sunset and slaughters the entire royal party! Even for Kate Nichols, this is a dramatically tragic ending. As a play *Zoroaster* would have been a nightmare to stage, as scene by scene the action flits between temple, palace and the monastery where Zoroaster goes on retreat. It ends with Zoroaster saying: 'When all things fall into their primal dross, and we stand face to face . . . with force supernal and Eternal Love.' It is another example of a Catherine Nichols moral — life after death will be happier by far than this earthly life, whether you are an English Christian, a Jewish princess or a magician in ancient Babylon!

Kate's final venture into print came in the form of a tale in the Christmas edition of the story magazine *Atalanta*, and is a fanciful piece called 'Tsi-te-see'. The Honourable Sophonisba nods off to sleep while drinking a cup of china tea and the 'spirit of the tea table' whisks her off to the Enchanted Land. In the Enchanted Land Sophonisba discovers that even elves and fairies make a mess of their love affairs — but on the way there are some amusing conceits and clever ideas. Tsi-te-see is a naughty fairy who wears a yellow paper dress but is constantly tearing it or getting it wet so she has to have new ones made by her unhappy mother, Sob-a-way. Tsi-te-see risks wearing out the tip of her pigtail by using it to sweep the floor, there are talking flowers, pink china palaces and a magic gum that makes the oars of boats stick to the water. There are young men dressed in suits of fine porcelain who have to be careful not to 'run up against each other, lest they should crack'. Kate almost pokes fun at herself and her previous writings.

> I shall not detain you for a moral, because in the Enchanted Land no-one is ever allowed to point a moral; they say that all pointed weapons are forbidden by the Mandarins, as being dangerous and likely to draw blood. So if you happen to be carrying a pointed remark about with you, and wish to get rid of it, you must climb over the Great Wall and call it out on the other side, then it is picked up by the birds and they build it into their nests, and then, when the rich Hung-Waks and Thik-Syds take their birds' nest soup, they swallow down the remark too, and being in a good temper, it doesn't do them any harm.

In many ways this little story is one of the best of Kate's writings, and it seems rather a pity that she did not indulge the lighter side of her imagination more often.

83. Bookplate Catherine Nichols
designed for the Bosworth Harcourt
bequest to Norwich Public Library.

84. Pencil sketch for a bookplate by Catherine Nichols.
In the Bosworth Harcourt collection in the Norfolk Record Office.

II

The George Borrow centenary and Kate Nichols, entrepreneur

Someone who did indulge his imagination at length was George Henry Borrow (1803–81). He was one of Norwich's more colourful adopted sons, an author, raconteur, consummate linguist, boxer, mystic, traveller and 'perhaps one of the handsomest men of his day'. His father was a Cornishman who joined the army to escape prosecution for a brawl in which his employer was seriously injured. George's mother came from Dereham. The family travelled extensively around the British Isles with the army, settling in Norfolk for a while when George was a boy and returning for good when he was a teenager and his father retired.

He seems to have been a precocious, solitary little boy with a gift for making odd friends, and at quite a young age he befriended a snake catcher who made him a present of a tamed and de-fanged adder to keep as a pet. When later on he met a group of gypsies, the fact that he could carry a snake about in his shirt without being bitten convinced the more superstitious of them that he was some sort of demi-god. They befriended him, he learnt their language and acquired a Romany 'blood brother', Ambrose Smith, and a bitter enemy in the old gypsy woman, Mrs Herne, who would later try to poison him. He described his experiences at length in his semi-autobiographical novel, *Lavengro*, published in 1851.

He had a chequered early career, including close friendships with two men who were later hanged for murder. One was a 12-year-old Scottish drummer boy in his father's regiment; the other was John Thurtell of Harford Hall Farm in Lakenham who taught Borrow to box. The Borrows spent time in Edinburgh and Ireland and

George discovered a gift for languages, learning Latin and Greek (presumably at school) and Irish. In 1814 the family were in Norwich. However ramshackle an upbringing they may have given their two boys, the parents obviously saw the value of education and young George Borrow was sent to the Norwich Grammar School alongside Kate's father and uncle. Fellow pupils remembered his gift for story-telling; between lessons he would gather three or four of his friends together and make up wild stories, doing rapid sketches of each of his characters as he talked.

By 1816, after further travels, the family were back in Norwich and George was back at school, receiving regular floggings from the choleric Edward Valpy and learning French and German from a disgraced priest from Caen University. When he left school Borrow was apprenticed to a firm of solicitors, Simpson and Rackham, for five years, a surprisingly sedate choice of career for a rackety young man. It did not suit him and he did not remain there after his apprenticeship ended. Meanwhile he had taught himself Danish, Old Norse and Welsh!

For some years he disappears from view, but in 1833 he got himself a job with the British and Foreign Bible Society, walking to the interview in London from Norwich in 27 hours and spending just 5½d (about 1p) on the journey. The next few years were spent translating the Bible into Russian, Spanish and Mandarin, travelling extensively and having numerous adventures. In 1840 he married Mary Clarke, a widow with a grown-up daughter, £450 a year and a cottage at Oulton. They lived there before spending time in Yarmouth and London and travelling around the UK. Mary Borrow died in 1860. George was cared for in old age by his step-daughter and her husband and died, back at Oulton, in 1881.[1]

****

85. *Catherine Maude Nichols' portrait of*
George Borrow,
copied from one painted by his brother,
John T. Borrow.

George was born in 1803, so the centenary of his birth was actually 1903, but it was not until 1913 that anyone in Norwich thought of commemorating it. By 1913, not only had George Borrow acquired a following of people who admired his books, they had also given themselves a name – 'the Borrovians'. 'The centenary of George Borrow's birth, in 1903, passed with little notice or celebration,' ran the 1913 commemorative booklet. 'As a result, a group of local Borrovians set up a committee to organise a major celebration in 1913.' The committee consisted of prominent people – the Lord Mayor of Norwich, the Dean of Norwich, William Jarrold, Herbert Jenkins and E. M. Beloc. Frank J. Farrell, a Yarmouth silk manufacturer, was appointed Honorary Secretary and was responsible for most of the planning.

On 1st April 1913 the antiquarian James Hooper wrote to Frank Farrell suggesting the production of some sort of souvenir book to mark the event.[2] There had been one for 'the Sir Thomas Browne occasion some years since, when Lord Avebury unveiled the statue, and it is a *possession.*' This is the same James Hooper whose widow Mrs Pym, Kate Nichols and their friends would later club together to support, 'a Bohemian of the Bohemians'[3] – and he was already strapped for cash. He expressed willingness to write the text but pointed out that in view of his straitened circumstances he would require a fee 'but nothing extravagant'. He also suggested that they approach Clement Shorter, the artist,

86. *Alfred Munnings' design for the cover of the*
George Borrow centenary souvenir booklet.

87. Etching of George Borrow's house by Catherine Maude Nichols for the George Borrow centenary souvenir booklet.

to produce illustrations for the volume. Shorter seems to have turned them down and the numerous illustrations that finally appeared in the volume were mostly photographic reproductions of paintings owned by a number of the 'Borrovians'. The cover showed Alfred Munnings' vision of George Borrow and his gypsy chum as young boys on a hillside overlooking the city of Norwich, and there is a series of Borrow-inspired poems by Reverend F. W. Orde Ward and Mr E. Peake.

No-one approached her, but Kate Nichols was determined to be a part of the 'centenary'. She offered the committee a series of her etchings of the interior of 'George Borrow's house'. In fact it was his parents' house where he had lived as a boy and young man before setting off on his wanderings. By 1913 the house had stood empty for many years so there is no furniture in any of Kate's pictures of its dark, mysterious, low ceilinged rooms. The etchings appear in the centenary souvenir, erroneously described as 'pen pictures'.

88. Etching of George Borrow's house by Catherine Maude Nichols for the George Borrow centenary souvenir booklet.

89. Etching of George Borrow's house by Catherine Maude Nichols for the George Borrow centenary souvenir booklet.

The main centenary celebrations took place on 5th July. There were guided tours of Borrow's House, a reception at St Andrew's Hall, performances by gypsy bands and dancers and a dinner at the Maid's Head. The guests were pictured in a 'flashlight photograph' to which they all added their signatures — this later hung in the Borrow Museum.[4] At the reception, the Lord Mayor, Arthur Samuelson, presented the deeds of 'George Borrow's house' in Willow Lane to the city.[5] It was to become a museum in Borrow's memory. Borrow's house remained a museum until 1948. It has since been demolished.[6]

Meanwhile, that July, Norwich Castle Museum put on an exhibition about George Borrow and amongst the exhibits was a

90. George Borrow's house, Willow Lane by Catherine Maude Nichols. Dry-point.

91. The mayoral party outside George Borrow's house in 1913.

picture of 'Marshland Shales' (a horse made famous in *Lavengro*) lent by the husband of Kate's school-friend, Mary Mann, and a portrait of Kate's father, William Peter Nichols, who had been at school with Borrow and had been his doctor. In a letter to his mother George once complained that he 'had been so physicked by Nichols that I could barely stand'.[7]

The Gypsy Club, based in London and consisting of people with an interest in the Romany way of life rather than gypsies themselves, laid on special excursion trains from London to Norwich, published a souvenir edition of their magazine, organised a camping and open air life exhibition on Mousehold Heath and ran a competition for people 'who obtain a living on the road'. This was to encourage the working classes to become hawkers and pedlars (getting a licence was recommended but not obligatory) so they could lead healthy lives in the fresh air! The reaction of the local authorities to this bizarre initiative is unrecorded.[8]

Kate had her own ideas about celebrating the centenary. As well as the etchings she produced for the souvenir booklet she made a copy of a portrait of George Borrow painted by his soldier brother, John, who had studied with Crome. Perhaps she thought that with Borrow so much in the news someone would be keen to buy it. A photograph of the original appears in the souvenir booklet and Kate's version is a good copy, but in its present form it appears to have suffered from later over-painting or clumsy restoration so that the young George Borrow now peers out at us through a tangle of muddy coloured draperies. It is in Norwich Castle Museum.

ORDER FORM.

To
                                    Bookseller, or Print Seller

Please reserve for me, and send as soon as published, the Portfolio of Etchings, entitled: "*HAUNTS OF GEORGE BORROW.*"

(a) .... cop .... *of general issue. Price £2 2s. net.*

(b) .... cop .... *ditto, special proofs on India paper, £4 4s. net.*

for which I enclose Cheque value £

    (*Signed*)

    Address

Published by JARROLD & SONS, Warwick Lane, London and Norwich.
N.B.—The Publishers must be immediately advised of this Order.

92. Order form for Catherine Nichols' folder of etchings produced to commemorate the George Borrow centenary.

Kate also produced a folder of four etchings, 'The Haunts of George Borrow', containing etchings of 'Borrow's House from Cow Hill', 'Borrow's House and Court', 'The city from George Borrow's window' and 'The staircase in Borrow's House'. The folder was produced by Jarrolds and retailed at two guineas, while the 50 sets of signed proofs on India paper were priced at four guineas each. The folder advertised Kate and her work.

> Artist, Miss C. M. Nichols RE, has kindly undertaken the Etchings. The merit and status of Miss Nichols are such as to need no comment. Suffice it to say that she is a Fellow of the Royal Society of Painter-Etchers, was the first lady ever elected a Fellow of that Society, and the only lady Fellow for ten years. Her work has been hung in the Royal Academy, London, the Paris Salon, Munich, Venice and elsewhere; and in addition to her English distinctions, she is also a member of a distinguished French Society. Sir Seymour Haden, Ex-president of the Painter-Etchers' Society, bought and presented to Norwich a number of her Etchings, so that her native city could possess a representative collection of her art.[9]

While Kate seems to have donated some of the proceeds of sales to the committee organising the celebrations she seems also to have made a reasonable profit for herself. On 2nd July 1913 she wrote to the organiser, Frank Farrell, a hasty letter in her large sprawling script. 'I've had such a truly *awful rush* or I could have sold more — I enclose a cheque for 12 shillings.' Was this, perhaps, 10% of six sales?[10]

Whether or not Kate made much money from the George Borrow Centenary, it is a fine example of her entrepreneurial approach and her determination that no artistic event in Norwich should pass without her intervention.

****

Speaking on the occasion of the presentation of her portrait to the museum in 1923, Prince Duleep Singh claimed 'Material affairs affected her not at all, and so long as she herself was satisfied with one of her pictures it was quite of secondary importance whether it won her money as well as fame. In fact money "filthy lucre" did not count!'[11] The press report suggests that at this point his audience applauded him with calls of 'Hear, hear'. Of course, it was not the done thing for artists to confess to any financial interest. In an interview for *The Girl's Realm* in April 1899, for example, Walter Crane, then head of the Royal College of Art, affected to be shocked by the very idea that an artist might set out to make money. 'Now Mr Crane' the interviewer had asked, 'will you tell me which branch of art taught here you would advise a girl to take up who had her own living to earn?' Mr Crane hesitated, and doodled on the pad before him for several minutes before replying. 'The idea of anyone working at art in order to make money is to me repulsive. I dislike the competition and hackwork which always results . . . you must realise that far better work is achieved when the greed, the desire of gain is non-essential, or at least in the background.' It was a suitably idealistic and unrealistic reply — and no doubt Kate, too, felt obliged to express total disinterest in what she was paid. But for someone who was so unconcerned about money, she certainly had sound business sense.[12]

As well as exhibiting in institutions where her work was on view to the general public she held numerous selling exhibitions in dealers' galleries. In London, Mr R. Gutekunst of 16 King Street, off St James's Square, apparently had a folio of her etchings 'permanently on view'[13] — and a number of the works in the Norwich Castle collection still bear his firm's stickers. In Norwich, Mr G. T. Dimmock held his first exhibition of work by Norfolk and Suffolk artists in 1883 and Kate was amongst the exhibitors.[14] He also published *Lines of Thought* for her. An advertisement in the *Eastern Daily Press* on Saturday 1st October 1910 urged readers to go to see 'Portraits in PASTEL by MISS FAITH K. BOSWELL and ETCHINGS by MISS C. M. NICHOLS at MISS BOSWELL'S STUDIO 43 LONDON STREET' between 11am and 5pm from October 3rd to the 15th.'

Kate also held exhibitions in her own studio. There was one in the last week of January 1899. 'The public have now the chance of inspecting over one hundred of Miss Nichols' best productions,' reported the *Norwich Chronicle* on 21st January, 'and the opportunity is being extensively taken advantage of, while the numerous visitors leave the studio with expressions of extreme satisfaction respecting the works they have seen. As a price, and a reasonable one withal, is affixed to each, it is doubtful whether the collection will again be seen intact, as the gems of the assemblage are bound to find purchasers. There are in the collection pictures to suit all tastes.' The journalist went on to list some of the pictures and Kate's 'best-sellers' — etchings of Cow Hill, Ber Street, Strangers' Hall and 'exquisite' ones of trees and woodland scenery were again on show. 'Miss Nichols places a completed and well-arranged catalogue in the hands of visitors, who receive a hearty welcome.'

She also produced hand-outs for visitors with quotations from a range of newspapers and magazines praising her work. Most of these quotes are undated

THE STUDIO,
73, SURREY STREET,
NORWICH.

PRESS NOTICES, Etc.

Miss Nichols, R.E., S.M., etc., is an artist well known in the Eastern Counties. She has been a frequent Exhibitor at the Royal Academy and in many of the London Galleries, as well as at St. Louis, Melbourne, Munich, Dresden, New Zealand, The Salon, Paris, 1907, and elsewhere.

When the Royal Society of Painter-Etchers was instituted, Miss Nichols was made a Fellow—the first Lady Fellow and the only one for some ten years.

Mr. R. Gutekunst, 16, King Street, St. James, London, has had permanently on view a Folio of Miss Nichols' " etched " work.

The following are extracts from the Press Notices of her Works:—

" Among the etchers of small landscapes few are more satisfactory than Mr. Oliver Hall, whose " Pine Trees on the edge of the Moor," (24) and half a dozen other plates are at once extremely delicate in their execution and telling in their effect. To the same class belongs the work of several ladies,   .   .   .   including Miss C. M. Nichols,   .   .   .   whose success is one of many proofs that in some branches of art women are becoming serious rivals of men."—The Times, Feb. 26th, 1906.

The Studio for Jan., 1907, reproduces two of Miss Nichols' dry-points. The full-page reproduction of " Cow-Hill, Norwich," being one of the two exhibited in The Salon of 1907. Commenting on these works The Studio remarks:—" The etchings of Miss C. M. Nichols have long been familiar to visitors to the exhibitions of the Royal Society of Painter-Etchers, of which society for ten years she remained the only lady member.   .   .   .   The etching of ' Oulton Broad,' which we reproduce, is also an example of her sense of style and gift for understanding the true qualities of the etched line."

" A couple of dry-points of rare excellence, by Miss C. M. Nichols, R.E."
                                                                    Daily Chronicle.

" Two Landscapes exhibited by Miss C. M. Nichols in the Royal Academy, ' Riverside, Norwich ' and ' Evening on the Broads,' were both exceedingly beautiful."
                                                                    The Queen.

" A remarkably clever collection of etchings by Miss Nichols, R.E   .   .   .   .   . A very short inspection of the work betrays the intensely artistic temperament of the artist. There is shewn in all a delightful absence of mannerism, and at the same time, taking the work en bloc, a curious inequality that, in spite of the ardent devotion to nature and true poetic feeling, seems the invariable accompaniment of the highest artistic natures."—The Lady.

" Full of delightful tone and skilful perspective."—Eastern Daily Press.

93. Handout produced to publicise Catherine Nichols' work.
Date unknown.

and so would be almost impossible to trace, but the sources ranged from *The Times, The Daily Telegraph* and *Daily News* to *The Queen, The Lady's Pictorial* and *The Illustrated London News*. There was even a quotation from *Jewish World* — but it is notable that there is only one brief quote from a Norwich paper: 'Full of delightful tone and skilful perspective — *Eastern Daily Press*'.[15] It is interesting to speculate how this hand-out was compiled. As far as we know, Kate did not have an agent, though creating such a collection of favourable notices would have been the sort of thing an agent would have done. Did friends send her press cuttings? Were there people in London scanning magazines and newspapers on her behalf? Was it done through the RSPE? We have no way of knowing.

Some of the same quotations — and others — appear on the cover of Kate's 1907 folder of etchings 'After Crome'. This was a more expensive offering than the George Borrow one — eight guineas for two large etchings on Japanese vellum, five guineas for a version on cheaper paper. The subjects she chose to etch were 'Poringland Oak' and 'Boulevard des Italiens'. Crome's original paintings of these subjects are now in the Tate and Norfolk Castle Museum respectively.

Kate Nichols explored every avenue she could think of to sell her work. She wrote books and poems, designed bookplates and had her poems set to music and sold as scores. Did she need the money or was she simply a businesswoman who could not pass up an opportunity when it presented itself? We cannot be sure. She certainly knew her market and had a good idea of what would sell — views of coast and countryside, picturesque townscapes, miniature and portrait commissions and the occasional copy of a work by or of someone famous. She experimented with composition, she etched views that were not conventionally scenic — barren empty landscapes and storm tossed fields — she flirted with painting in the Impressionist style; but she never lost sight of her audience and what they would buy and she seldom produced work that was too extreme for their taste.

94. *'Poringland oak' after Crome from Kate's 1907 folder of etchings after Crome.*

12

Elisabetta[1]

Both Lilly Bull and Mary Mann wrote of Catherine Nichols' willingness to help people she saw as deserving or interesting, regardless of their background. We know about Alastor the Palmist, but the only other documented case we have is that of Elisabetta Marcantonio.

Elisabetta was Italian and she was about nine years old and playing the accordion on the streets of Norwich when Kate met her. The little girl had been born in 1869 in, or near the small town of Picinisco in Lazio, which lies about 75 miles east of Rome, surrounded by hills, on the edge of what is now the Abruzzi National Park. Her father, Gesidio Marcantonio, was the younger son of a local landowner, but he had six brothers and his inheritance was very small and this led to family quarrels. The local priest heard of someone who was offering work in England and so, unbelievable as it sounds today, Gesidio left his wife, Maria, and their three young daughters, and taking their eldest child, Elisabetta, set off with the 'padroni' or master and a band of a dozen youngsters to walk to England. They slept in barns and hedgerows and the only food they had on the journey was bread (for which they were each allowed a halfpenny a day) and whatever they could forage or beg. Elisabetta remembered how a French woman had given them a bullock's heart and how her father showed her how to cook it on a stick over an open fire; she remembered sleeping huddled together with all the others in an open barn on a bitterly cold, snowy night, but there must have been many other hardships. The journey took three months.

The padroni paid their boat fares from Calais to Dover and the ragged group walked on to London. There he provided them with accordions — which none of them could play — and sent them out to beg on the streets, wearing brightly coloured ribbons and headscarves. It is difficult to believe that street musicians could ever have earned enough to justify the expense of the master's journey to Italy to find them, or to make the long, arduous journey home on foot worthwhile, but by the 1870s, when Elisabetta and her father set out, the 'trade' in Italian child musicians was well-established and, apparently, quite lucrative.

Italian children were a common sight on English streets throughout the nineteenth century; some sang, some played musical instruments, some had small animals which they showed off to passers-by, others had boxes of 'curiosities' which they would open and display for a small fee. The smaller the child the more likely they were to win the sympathy of their audience and the more money they could make. Most of the children came from impoverished rural districts, and no doubt parents struggling to feed large families felt they were giving at least one of their offspring the chance of a better life. Italian children were also a common sight on the streets of Paris and New York and other large cities in Europe and America. The padrone would give his charges some basic musical instruction — presumably some evidence of musical ability was a prerequisite to being selected for the journey — and in return he would set them up on a particular 'beat' which long experience had shown was a good place to make money. The children served an informal apprenticeship for a set period — usually three years — and during that time the padroni fed, clothed and housed them and took all the money they earned.

Opinions about the lives of the little street musicians vary. J.Thomson and Adolphe Smith wrote *Street Life in London* in 1876–77 and present quite a rosy picture. They admitted that it would be a good thing if British legislation about child labour also applied to foreign children, and felt it would be preferable for the children to be in school, but they pointed out that conditions in Italy were so bad that the little Italians were probably better off in London than they would have been at home. They acknowledged that some padroni may have ill-treated their charges, that the children's living conditions were often squalid and that they were not always well fed, but 'Their pockets are full of pence. What system of control can prevent them from buying food in the streets where they play?' — and for children prepared to risk a beating if they were found out, this was probably true. They commented on the healthy appearance of the children, and added, 'there is an element of romance about the swarthy Italian youth to which the English poor cannot aspire. Then there is something irresistible in the bright glitter of his eyes, in his cheerful gait, and his fascinating manners.' They also felt that the children, living with the padroni in the heart of the Italian community, were probably relatively safe because the Italians were well-known for their love of children and neighbours would have sounded the alarm if they feared for the children's welfare. Besides, they argued, many of the Italians were in touch with families back home. They sent money home and the more successful ones often returned to Italy for the winter — if the little street musicians were routinely abused, news would filter back to their communities and other parents would be unwilling to entrust their offspring to a padrone promising them a better life in a cold, grey, faraway country. Other authors were less sanguine and quoted cases of serious ill treatment.[2] Elisabetta was obviously luckier than most because she had her father with her — though even he was not always able to protect her, as we shall see.

After a time, Elisabetta and Gesidio were brought to Norfolk — we are not told what happened to the others who had travelled with them but perhaps they were passed on to other padroni in other cities. The master continued to take most of their earnings and on one occasion accused her — wrongly — of stealing £2 and beat her severely, which entirely destroyed any residual sense of loyalty to him that she might have felt. He apologised but it was too late. She determined to get her own back and the following day, when she was taken to Aldeburgh to work, she earned the few shillings that she thought would satisfy him and then simply went and sat on the beach for the day!

We have no pictures of the little girl that Kate befriended, but photos of Elisabetta as an old lady show a thin-faced woman with a large, beaky nose not unlike Kate Nichols' own. One wonders if the plain, plucky little girl reminded Kate of herself at the same age. Certainly she continued to look after Elisabetta

95. 'Elisabetta Capaldi', oil painting by Catherine Maude Nichols c.1900.
Reproduced by kind permission of the Carrara family.

for many years, taking the child with her to visit well-to-do friends in big houses around Norwich and acting almost as a surrogate mother. 'Miss Nichols and the other big families were never ashamed of Liz in her hobnailed boots,' Elisabetta remembered gratefully. We are told by Elisabetta's descendants that Kate drew and painted portraits of the girl — but none can be traced. (It is just possible that the engraving of 'The Musician' that Kate exhibited at the Norwich Art Circle Black and White exhibition in March 1907 is of Elisabetta or a member of her family, but we cannot be sure). Gesidio seems to have returned to Italy for a time while Elisabetta was still a young teenager; we do not know whether he took her with him or left her to fend for herself, but we do know that his wife gave birth to two more daughters, in Italy, in 1883 and 1884 respectively. It may be that it was after the birth of the youngest one that Gesidio brought Maria and their five other little girls to England. The family's fortunes appear to have improved. They had served out their term with the padrone and acquired a barrel organ. Elisabetta would sing along to the tunes it played and she and her father were the family's chief breadwinners.

Thomson and Smith were obviously impressed by the frugality and hard work of the Italian immigrants and contrasted them favourably with the English. 'They find that a beggar in England is richer than a labourer in Italy, and if they be not equally prosperous it is because he is not equally abstemious and economical. The Italian, therefore, migrates with the knowledge that he may rely on the generosity of the English, and that, if he only receives as much as many of the English poor, he may hope to save enough to buy himself a farm in his own country.' This may have been Gesidio's original plan, but it would appear that by the mid-1880s he had changed his mind and decided to bring his entire family to settle in England.

In 1886 he made another trip home to Italy and seems to have arranged a marriage for Elisabetta with Luigi Capaldi, the son of a landowner in Picinisco. By this time the family were living in Ipswich and Maria had just given birth to her seventh child and first son, whom they named Sidney. It seems that Gesidio was known as 'Sid' in England and the boy was given the English version of his father's nickname. Gesidio Marcantonio made it home to Ipswich and his family — but he died a few days later. With her father dead, the family returned to Norwich and Elisabetta went to beg help from Catherine Nichols who had been so kind to her when she was younger. Kate does not seem to have failed her. The family settled in one of the yards off Ber Street, not far from where Kate lived, and Elisabetta, now helped by her sister Luizia, continued to work as a street musician to support their mother and the five younger children.

Mariners Lane and the yards off Ber Street were home to Norwich's Italian community. The 1891 census tells us that the Ferri family, the Gallos, the Gillys,

96. 'Ber Street', 1878 by Catherine Maude Nichols. Dry-point. The courts off Ber Street and
Mariner's Lane were where most of Norwich's Italian community lived.
This image was exhibited at the Royal Academy in 1879.

the Mancinis, the Nobles, the Yannittis, and the Tartaglis all lived in the area. The Marcantonios probably knew them all. The Gallos were labourers and the Ferris were ice cream makers; the Gillys, Mancinis, Yanittis and Tartaglis were all street musicians like Elisabetta and Luizia. It is astonishing that they could all make a living in a city the size of Norwich, but it seems that they did.

Two years after Gesidio's death — by which time Elisabetta had probably all but forgotten her father's talk of her marriage — Luigi Capaldi arrived, unannounced, to claim his bride. Elisabetta had little choice but to marry him, and Kate Nichols paid for the couple to have a fashionable wedding at St John Maddermarket Catholic Chapel. The service was in Italian and the couple were both dressed in their national costume — Elisabetta's dress was blue silk with white muslin and a tulle veil, and Kate lent her a diamond bracelet for the occasion. Hundreds of people came to watch the wedding and the police had to be brought in to control the crowds which stretched all the way back to the market place. However, despite their brief taste of fame, the couple continued to earn their livings as street musicians, pushing their organ through the streets in all weathers and singing Italian songs. It was a far harder life than Luigi could ever have envisaged. He had been raised a gentleman, but presumably, like Gesidio before him, he did not inherit enough to support a wife. In time he and Elisabetta had two daughters, but the English climate did not suit him and he died of TB in 1902. He left his wife £218 4s 7d — not a king's ransom but nonetheless a significant sum for a working family.

In 1903, Elisabetta married again, this time, as far as we know, without the help of Kate Nichols. Nonetheless, the wedding took place in what is now the Catholic cathedral. Elisabetta's second husband was another Italian, Leonello Carrara, originally a plaster image maker from Lucca, and they had four children. Elisabetta seems to have continued to ply her trade as a street musician, sometimes helped by her husband, but Leonello also seems to have been something of an entrepreneur. He went to America for a time and, according to family legend, Elisabetta was supposed to follow him but she had a bad dream about the voyage which she took as a warning and cancelled her passage. The ship she was to have taken was the *Titanic*. No doubt Kate Nichols would have seen her as 'an eerie' and been profoundly impressed.

Leonello returned from America and the couple stayed in Norwich, and in their later years they followed that most Italian of occupations — ice cream making. It may sound as if Elisabetta found herself a rather less arduous trade for her old age, but Thomson and Smith dispel that illusion in their chapter on 'Halfpenny Ices'. They write of ice cream makers buying their ice at 4 in the morning and their milk an hour or so later so as to have the ices ready to sell on the streets by the time children were going to school. The most lucrative ices were the water

97. The Carrara ice cream cart, early twentieth century.

ices, what we would call ice lollies — made from water coloured with cochineal for raspberry or water with a little lemon essence for lemon flavour. 'Cream' ices contained milk and some egg — but the mark-up on the ingredients was still high. Once made, the ices were sold on the streets from a barrow. Perhaps the Carraras' ice cream cart and the barrel organ toured the streets together.

Kate Nichols continued to interest herself in Elisabetta, and in the early 1900s she painted a — rather unflattering — portrait of her which is still in the family. Kate also mentioned her in her will as one of a handful of friends to whom she wished to leave a keepsake. However, she calls her 'Elizabeth Capaldi'. The Anglicisation of the Christian name is understandable — Elisabetta was always

98. 'Black Anna', Elisabetta's daughter, who ran the Jolly Butcher public house. Reproduced by kind permission of Maddie Bartle.

known as 'Liz' — but she had been 'Mrs Carrara' for almost twenty years. It is hard to know whether this was an example of Kate's failing memory (like her inclusion in the will of Albon Powell, her dead nephew) or whether she had seen so little of Elisabetta since Luigi's death that she was unaware she had remarried.

Leonello Carrara died in 1944; Elisabetta survived him by a decade. She was interviewed by the *Eastern Daily Press* in 1949; over 25 years after Kate Nichols' death, Elisabetta was still loud in her praise. This was one of Kate's protégées who was genuinely grateful for the help she had received.

13

The NAVS

It was not just human waifs and strays who tugged at Kate Nichols' heart strings. She was almost irrationally fond of animals.

We do not know whether the Nichols family kept pets. There would have been horses, of course — Dr Nichols had a carriage and a resident groom and it is likely that the family had at least one other vehicle for Matilda and the children to use — but we do not know whether they had pet dogs and cats, canaries or any of the other small caged creatures children delight in keeping. Dr Nichols was a countryman, a farmer's son and a surgeon — he was probably not a sentimental pet owner — but of his wife we know nothing. Perhaps it was she who encouraged her daughter's love of animals. Perhaps as an only child (for the first nine years of her life) Kate relied on pets, real or imaginary, for company. What we do know is that once she had her own establishment, Kate filled her studio with creatures — not lapdogs and pussycats but pet mice and rabbits which ran loose about her rooms. Her maid was even forbidden to knock down cobwebs for fear of disturbing the spiders — and perhaps the delicate outlines of the webs appealed to Kate the etcher. Kate's particular favourite was a pet rat which travelled everywhere with her in her muff — even to church — and which she believed to be so sympathetic to her moods that when she was unhappy it would sit on her shoulder and cry![1] Such sentimentality and anthropomorphism were not uncommon amongst well-to-do ladies — Kate's friend Mary Mann and her daughters were besotted with their pets — dogs, ponies, cats and Poddles the much-loved parrot who pecked visitors' ankles and had an embarrassingly colourful vocabulary[2] — but it was at odds with the way the majority of Victorians viewed the animal kingdom.

In one of Mary Mann's novels, *Rose at Honeypot*, a young gentlewoman takes lodgings with a village family and is appalled by the cruelty of the husband and his small son. Four year old Alick is a little monster who enjoys spearing live insects on pins to see them run round and round in desperate circles. He was only just prevented from putting the kitten in the cooking pot, he lobs stones at the gamekeeper's dog tethered in her kennel and, to his father's profound admiration, he once plucked a live robin. 'That was a master one, that was!' [Mr Jaggard] cried proudly. 'He'd plucked'm as clane as a whustle, Alick had. I'm blamed ef he weren't a hoppin' round, a mask o' blood, when I come home; and Alick a'screechin' wi' laughin." When Rose remonstrates with the boy's mother she is truculent. 'It's not as if they was *human*,' she says. It seems likely that Mary Mann knew of a child who did pluck a live bird — the incident reappears in another novel, *Astray in Arcady*, and we know most of Mary Mann's novels were based on real people and events.[3]

Such cruelty was accepted because most people did not see animals as sentient beings. Farm animals were there to milk, shear or slaughter and eat. Dogs and horses were machines to herd sheep, catch rats or pull heavy loads. Wild creatures were there to be shot for sport or poached for food. And if anyone doubted this, the Bible was explicit: 'Then God said "Let us make man in our image, according to our likeness; and let him have dominion over the fish of the sea and over the birds of the heavens and over the cattle and over all the earth and over every creeping thing that creeps upon the earth"' (Genesis 1:26). In a country where working men could lose their jobs at a moment's notice, where large numbers went hungry, ill shod and poorly clad, where many children worked for long hours at dangerous trades or were sadistically beaten at school and at home, most people did not see the suffering of animals as a priority — or even as a problem. Nonetheless, the Society for the Prevention of Cruelty to Animals had been founded in 1824, established by a group of 22 reformers led by Richard Martin MP, William Wilberforce MP and the Reverend Arthur Broome in the aptly named 'Old Slaughter's Coffee House' in St Martin's Lane, near the Strand. The foundation is marked by a plaque on the modern day building at 77–78 St Martin's Lane. It was the first animal welfare charity in the world and in its first year brought 63 offenders before the courts. In 1840 Queen Victoria granted the society royal status and it became the Royal Society for the Prevention of Cruelty to Animals — as it is today.

By the time Kate Nichols was a mature woman, court cases for acts of cruelty towards animals were common and records in the library[4] in Norwich contain gruesome details of some of the cases tried there; and there were 22 other courts spread right across Norfolk so this only hints at the total scale of suffering and prosecutions. The following list, c. 1896, gives just a glimpse of what was being brought to court. Some, like shooting a cat in the eye or cutting off its tail, smack of deliberate and malicious cruelty but others were probably a response to the frustration and desperation that famers and labourers felt as they tried to scrape a living during an ever-deepening agricultural depression.

Analysis of Convictions

Animals	Cruelty	Number of convictions
Horses	Working in an unfit state	73
	Kicking, beating etc.	26
	Travelling unharnessed when lame	13
	Stabbing with a hay fork	1
	Starving by withholding food	2
	Riding with sore back	1
	Over driving	1

Another page gave details of two of these cases:

(i) A farmer caused a mare to be in a field searching for food when incurably lame from cankered feet; one of the hooves on a fore foot was sloughing off from the disease and bleeding. The Mare groaned at every step.

(ii) A Parish clerk starved his pony; it got so emaciated and exhausted that it had to be put into slings; it was afterwards removed to be better cared for and had to be bodily lifted into a cart by some men.

The list continued:

Donkeys	Working in an unfit state	1
	Beating and kicking	3
	Stabbing with a knife	1
Bullocks	Prodding where a horn had been removed	1
	Beating and kicking	3
Sheep	Driving cart over body and legs	1
	Kicking to death	1
Pigs	Over-crowding in carts	3
Dogs	Strangling	1

Shooting cruelly		I
Beating and kicking		2

A Gamekeeper beat his dog for half an hour with a heavy stick and afterwards with a pair of tongs. He then tied it behind his cart and dragged it along the road and finally hung it on a tree.

	Cutting tail off cruelly when alive	I
Cats	Stoning	I
	Cutting tail off when alive	I
	Beating and kicking	I
	Shooting in the eye	I

These are just a few of the 198 offences listed.

Another list recorded the fine or other punishment imposed on an individual. The occupation is recorded but not the name.

Laundryman	Working horse unfit	13s 0d
Corn dealer	ditto	13s 0d
Hawker	Unfit travelling donkey	5s 0d
Drover	Driving sheep lame	£1 0s 0d
Farm Bailiff	Causing sheep to be driven lame	£7 1s 6d
Dealer	Working horse unfit	16s 0d
Labourer	Beating a horse	5s 0d
Fish Hawker	Working a horse unfit	£1 18s 6d
Foreman Drover	Prodding a bullock	£2 17s 6d
Farmer	Working a horse – unfit	£1 10s 0d
Soldier	Beating a pony	One month's hard labour
Gypsy	Starving, working and beating a horse	One month's hard labour

Many cases concerned horses. Working horses were often cruelly ill-treated. Reputable firms looked after their animals well, but the real problems came when the animals were too old to give of their best. Then they were sold, often at knock down prices, to small tradesmen who could not afford better beasts. The horses ended their days over worked and underfed, their injuries unattended to. In towns up and down the country the sight of old working horses collapsing and dying in the street was not uncommon.

Riding and carriage horses were also often abused – their treatment was highlighted in *Black Beauty* written by Norfolk-born author Anna Sewell and published in 1877. Kate Nichols may even have known her as in the 1870s Anna

Sewell lived just outside Norwich in the village of Old Catton. Anna was an invalid and had difficulty walking so she often travelled by carriage — which probably explains her great love of horses and concern for their welfare. Her book became a classic and had an enormous effect on people's attitudes to their horses and ponies.

Towards the end of the nineteenth and the beginning of the twentieth century increasing numbers of middle and upper class ladies (and a few men) were becoming concerned at the cruelty animals suffered and were giving voice to their feelings. Kate Nichols was one such. Her alter ego, Judy Harrison in Mary Mann's story 'The Eerie', is portrayed as an animal lover and was constantly telling the police about men she saw ill-treating their animals. 'A score of [policemen] had, at different times, been forced by her, wildly gesticulating and raging in the streets, to take names and addresses of owners of horses unfit to be driven, to rescue dogs from masters who insufficiently fed them, cats who were ill-used'[5] — obviously Mary Mann is presenting an exaggerated picture but one suspects the police may have come to know Kate rather well for similar reasons. She was a strong minded woman and not one to remain silent in the face of wrongdoing. Like many of her friends Kate supported the RSPCA with an annual subscription, as a list of subscribers in Norwich Library shows. For how many years she did this we have no way of telling as the lists in the library only cover a very short period, but 'Nichols, Miss C. M.' is there with 10s 6d beside her name. Donations varied from as little as a shilling to £10. In 1896 a Ladies' Committee was formed and through their efforts extra subscriptions were raised; they were also responsible for starting groups throughout the county which, by 1916, as the balance sheet below shows, were very well established.

Receipts	£	s	d	Expenditure	£	s	d
Donations General Fund	240	8	1	Printing		7	4
Aylsham	5	18	6	Ambulance	377	7	6
Coltishall	1	19	6	Sent to Headquarters			
Dereham	13	8	4	Cheque Book	359	12	
Downham Market	25	13	5				
Fakenham	1	12	6				
Harleston	1	1	6				
Hunstanton	15	1	0				
Kenninghall	2	0	2				
North Walsham	16	6	4				
Saxlingham	11	3	1				
Swaffham	10	12	0				

Thetford	3	11	7
Walsingham and Wells	13	7	9
Wroxham	3	14	3
Balance in Hand	£ 12	5	3
Total	371	18	0

Audited and found correct 20th April 1916 – J. T. Todd

As well as money spent on tending sick, ill-treated and wounded animals in veterinary surgeries and prosecuting offenders, the RSPCA also spent money on ambulances for horses that were injured in the fighting in France.

Alongside the RSPCA another organisation, Our Dumb Friends' League (now the Blue Cross), was established in 1897 'for the encouragement of kindness to animals'[6] and in its early years it too was particularly concerned with horses, setting up a fleet of 'horse ambulances' to collect injured and dying animals from the streets and rescuing horses from the battlefields of the First World War. It would appear that Kate Nichols had some links with that organisation too, as in the early 1900s her protégé, Alastor the Palmist, performed at a fund raiser for the League at a garden party in Slough. It seems highly likely that Kate Nichols put his name forward.[7]

Birds and animals were also abused in the name of sport. Well-to-do Victorian

99. Horse ambulance as used in the First World War.

landowners spent much of their time hunting, shooting and fishing and they killed birds on an almost industrial scale — it was not unusual for a weekend's 'sport' to result in several thousand brace of dead birds. Many women hunted and some went shooting with their husbands — and most accepted it as an integral part of English rural life. But not everyone approved of blood sports and it would seem that women were more vocal than men in their condemnation. Kate very probably agreed with them — her friend Mary Mann certainly did.

Whilst researching some of the Braye papers[8] in Leicestershire Record Office some years ago we came across a lovely story which illustrates very clearly what many women were feeling.

The story was written in February 1863 for Fanny Wyatt-Edgell, eldest child of Reverend Edgell Wyatt-Edgell who lived at Stanford Hall with his family. Fanny, who was born in 1845, had three younger brothers, Henry, Alfred and Edmund. She had a close and loving relationship with all her family including her aunts and grandmother with whom she corresponded frequently; she visited them in London and Ireland. Many of these letters can still be seen in the Braye Papers in Leicestershire County Record Office. It was one of her Aunts, Louisa, who wrote this story for Fanny and her brothers. It may seem rather a strange tale to send to a young women who was already 18 years old, but perhaps Aunt Louisa had a hidden agenda. Fanny was due soon to 'come out' and be presented at court, the main aim of which, for young women, was to attract a suitable husband and marry well. For her family this was highly desirable as money was in fairly short supply.

If one element in Aunt Louisa's story was to urge Fanny to marry well and secure for herself a comfortable house and lifestyle, the other was to urge her to espouse the anti-hunting lobby, and from this point of view the story has considerable interest.

Fairy stories shuffled into the nineteenth century under a cloud. They were denounced as 'perfectly useless trumpery' by such as Mrs Trimmer writing in *The Guardian of Education*.[9] She denounced them as filling the heads of impressionable children with 'nonsense and fantasy instead of sound religious principles'. But fairy tales and folk tales are too potent a force to be suppressed and as the century progressed the tone against them softened as opponents came to see that they could be used as vehicles for imparting the solid Christian principles so dear to their hearts. Aunt Louisa was treading a well-worn path but following her own agenda. In her story, the little girl of the house befriends a fox and rescues him from baying hounds by hiding him in her room. When they have gone he takes her back to his 'home' and gives her a chest full of precious things which, he says, will come in useful for her forthcoming presentation at court. The fairy story follows the time-honoured course: Fanny meets a prince, the jewels in the casket the fox has given her are priceless and somehow he (the fox) manages to be presented at court at the very time she is there and is seated next to Queen Victoria. Of course he bends the Queen's ear about all the awful things that hunters do and the Queen responds by assuring him that she will become the patron of the society for the prevention of cruelty to animals. The story ends with Sir Renard, as he now is, returning home and saying:

> If the hounds come tomorrow and tear me to pieces, nothing will remain
> — whilst the promise that I took the opportunity of obtaining from Queen
> Victoria to become Patroness of the Society for the Prevention Of Cruelty to
> Animals will alleviate the sufferings of my fellow creatures, and be the glory
> of the nineteenth century after she and I have been removed to higher and
> happier pastures.

Aunt Louisa's views on hunting are thus made crystal clear and one suspects that Fanny was of like mind, for she had very definite ideas on moral and religious matters, as letters between her and her father clearly show. She leant towards Catholicism which was anathema to him. In the end, to the consternation and despair of the entire family, Fanny did not marry into wealth but confounded them all by taking the veil. There is another parallel here; Kate Nichols also became a Catholic, though not a nun.

We do not know what Kate thought of hunting and shooting, but her childhood friend, Mary E. Mann, the novelist, wrote at least two short stories about the cruelty of shooting. In 'Queen of the Pheasants' a little girl is often taken to see the pheasant chicks being reared on her father's estate. She is tender-hearted and cannot bear the thought of them being shot — and one night she has a dream in which she leads all the young pheasants to a magic land, away from the guns; she is their queen and they all live happily. However, reality asserts itself the next morning as her father and his friends ready themselves for a day's shooting — but mindful of the child's feelings, her governess takes her away for the day so she does not have to witness the carnage and carries on believing the birds are safe in the imaginary paradise she created for them in her dream. In another story, 'Blazing Away at the Birds', an inexperienced young townsman joins his friends to shoot but is so inept that he shoots one of his friends by accident — one gets the impression that Mary Mann thought this a form of poetic justice. The incident is based on reality; one of her neighbours accidentally shot and blinded a fellow sportsman.[10]

We do know that Kate Nichols was violently opposed to another form of animal cruelty that was gaining prominence in the late nineteenth century — vivisection. Animal experiments were often carried out in public, ostensibly for scientific purposes, and some onlookers were appalled by what they saw.

Prior to the passage of the 1876 Cruelty to Animals Act, animal welfare groups tested the limits of the existing 1822 Martin's Act for its efficiency in regulating vivisection. Under John Colam, the secretary of the RSPCA who was leading the charge for improved animal welfare, the 1874 meeting of the British Medical Association in Norwich provided an opportunity to demonstrate the vital need for new legislation.

Dr Eugene Magnan, a French physiologist, had been invited to lecture on the effects of alcohol. Included in his lecture was a demonstration of epilepsy in dogs being caused by the intravenous injection of alcohol and absinthe into a dog's leg — though what bearing this had on the human consumption of alcohol it was impossible to see. The reaction of the audience at his lecture was immediate. Medical members disrupted the experiment, the President of the Royal College of Surgeons from Ireland rushing forward and cutting the restraints of one of the two dogs being used in the experiment and calling the County Magistrate.

The subsequent RSPCA enquiry led to charges of wanton cruelty under Martin's Act being brought against Magnan and the English scientists who were supporting him. The resulting trial in December of that year did not find against the English scientists and no punishment was given to Magnan — but the legal wrangle did show how limited was the protection the Act gave when it came to using animals for unjustifiable medical experiments — and the cruelty involved. Press coverage of the trial aroused significant public interest and one month after the trial Frances Power Cobbe (an Irish anti-vivisection activist) called for the RSPCA to demand that parliament look again at vivisection and act against it. She raised a petition of over 600 names including many prominent people, amongst them Alfred Lord Tennyson, Lord Chief Justice Coleridge, Robert Browning and the Archbishops of York and Westminster. She also founded the National Anti-Vivisection Society.[11]

A small book in the local history section of Norwich Millennium Library,[12] published by Robert Harwick of Piccadilly, London in 1875, price twopence, records, verbatim, the case tried in Norwich Town Hall. It makes very grim reading. The language is not the same as we would use today — some words have different meanings now — but what was being said is all too clear. Five men were accused of taking part in the experiment resulting in cruelty to two dogs on the afternoon of 15th August in the smoking room of the Masonic Hall in Norwich. Only three were present at the court hearing — the other two were in Paris 'for the benefit of their health'. However, in spite of their absence, the magistrate in charge

decided to continue with the case. After much legal wrangling by the defence to
have the case adjourned or thrown out, the first witness, Mr Knight Brace, son of
the late Lord Justice, was called, sworn in and examined by Mr Colam.

> Q. On the 15th of August last you were in the Smoking Room of the Masonic
> Hall at 2pm.
> A. I was.
> Q. Tell us what you saw.
> A. There were two foreigners, one of them I believe Dr Magnan.
> Q. How was he dressed?
> A. I really forget how he was dressed, I fancy he had an apron on and his
> sleeves were tucked up. He was gesticulating very much. There was a dog on
> the table and seemed to be crucified to the board. In fact there were two dogs
> laid out by the legs tied with tape.
> Q. Were the mouths tied?
> A. Yes the poor dogs' mouths were tied, the wretches had fortified themselves
> in that manner.
> Q. What do you mean by that?
> A. Cruel people are naturally cowards and they had fortified themselves
> against the dogs in that manner.

The witness went on to relate how he saw tubes being forced into the dogs'
legs and a great deal of blood spilling out and a group of young men standing
round the table watching. The dogs, which were not anaesthetised, had their gall
bladders removed and slit open on the table; they were injected with all sorts of
substances, some of which were said to cure snake bites — though they had not
been bitten by snakes. Page after page of detail follows from different witnesses
and evaluations by medical professors as to the value of what was being done in
the name of science: all agreed it was of no medical use whatsoever.

As a result, Queen Victoria sent a carefully worded letter to the RSPCA
voicing her concern that unnecessary cruelty to animals was still being inflicted
in the name of science and hoping that education would eradicate it. In 1876
the Cruelty to Animals Act was passed to regulate animal experimentation.[13] It
established the principles that the benefits of an experiment should outweigh
the suffering caused, and that vivisection should no longer be a public spectacle
in which surgeons and other scientists demonstrated their speed and manual
dexterity. Vivisection now required three licences — one for the vivisector, one
for the establishment where it was practised and one for the type of experiment.
However, information about who was licensed to do what where was deliberately

kept secret to protect the scientists, and though inspectors were appointed there were not many of them and vivisection continued largely unchecked behind closed doors. Not for nothing did opponents of the bill describe it as the 'Vivisectionists' Charter'.

Some people still considered the very idea of regulation ridiculous. An undated poem in Norfolk Record Office, penned and read out at some — unspecified — Norwich society put this point of view in 14 verses of doggerel. Here are three of them.

> He was quite ready to admit a dog
> May have some sense of torture when you spike it,
> At which we did not wonder but a frog
> He somehow seemed to think might like it . . .
>
> One speaker could not say if frogs delight
> To yield their living innards to inspection,
> He'd never been one and they hadn't quite ·
> So good a claim as dogs for our protection . . .
>
> The president remarked his female friends
> Had signed in scores a marvellous petition,
> And for the better furthering of their ends
> Had prayed the queen to cause an abolition.[14]

That petition was presented to Queen Victoria in 1896 and Kate Nichols was probably one of the signatories. Her father, of course, had been a surgeon, and for much of his working life would have carried out operations without anaesthetic on human patients — which puts the controversy into some sort of perspective.

The anti-vivisection movement gained in strength after the 'brown dog affair' in February 1903 when William Bayliss performed a series of experiments on a hapless little brown terrier before an audience of 60 medical students at University College London. Bayliss claimed the dog was adequately anaesthetised — some Swedish women activists who had infiltrated the lecture claimed it was awake and struggling. Bayliss — a reputable scientist whose work on dogs discovered the existence of hormones — sued for libel and won, but the affair caused public outrage and there ensued pitched battles between the police and medical students protesting their right to learn. In 1906 a statue of the dog was erected by activists, with the inscription 'Men and women of England, how long shall these things be?' This was regularly vandalised by outraged medical students and for a time the statue had to have a police guard. In 1907 clashes between medical students and anti-vivisectionists led to the so-called 'brown dog riots', and feelings continued to run high for some years.[15] The publicity surrounding this episode may be what caused Kate Nichols to become more seriously involved with the anti-vivisection lobby.

We know that in 1909 she became president of the newly-formed Norwich branch of the 'Anti-vivisection Society'[16] but unfortunately no papers survive so we do not know what impact she had or for how long she remained president. In 1897 Frances Power Cobbe, who was by then in her mid-70s, fell out with the leaders of the National Anti-Vivisection Society that she had founded 20 years earlier and founded another society in opposition — the British Union for the Abolition of Vivisection.[17] The NAVS was pragmatic; it recognised that some animal experimentation was inevitable and might even be useful, and sought simply to regulate it and reduce the suffering of the animals involved. The BUAV under Miss Cobbe opposed all forms of vivisection and its stated mission was to bring all experimentation on animals to an end.

We do not know which course Kate Nichols favoured but her obituaries stress her on-going concern for animal welfare. On her death in 1923, for example, the *Eastern Daily Press* reported: 'Her sympathy with the sufferings to which animals are subjected through the ignorance and cruelty of human beings was very intense and practical. She was most zealous in the cause of anti-vivisection, and did all she could against the traffic of worn-out horses and other forms of cruelty. The animals have certainly lost a very good friend by her death.'[18]

The RSPCA, the Blue Cross (formerly Our Dumb Friends' League), NAVS and BUAV are all still in existence alongside a host of newer animal charities, and over the years new legislation to protect animals has been enacted, but sadly cruelty to animals is still with us.

EPILOGUE

Kate Nichols, Judy Harrison and Mary Mann's 'The Eerie'

Judy Harrison in Mary Mann's story 'The Eerie' was also deeply concerned about the suffering of animals, and it is clear that the character is based on Kate Nichols. Her protégé, Alastor the Palmist, appears as 'The Great Cavassa'. Of course it is only a story. It cannot be taken as an entirely reliable description of Kate Nichols — or Alastor — though we do know that many of Mary Mann's characters were libellously close to the real people on whom she based them.[1]

Judy Harrison's rapid speech and her habit of emphasising words tallies with Lilly Bull's description of Kate Nichols' speech, and with what we can deduce from her later letters which are full of emphatic under-linings. It seems likely that Judy's flamboyant 'un-English' gestures were also based on Kate. 'Judy' was christened Judith but preferred the short form of her name: Catherine Nichols' friends all called her 'Kate' or 'Katy' and that is how she appears in Mary Mann's letters and Bertie Mann's diary even when she was in her 60s, though in most other written sources she was a formal 'Miss C. M. Nichols'. Kate was dark haired and sallow skinned, though whether she was really as tanned as a red Indian — or, indeed, whether Mary Mann had ever seen a red Indian — is questionable. The description of Judy wearing black with touches of bright colour to enhance her raven black hair is echoed in the 1943 description of Kate in the *Eastern Daily Press*[2] — if Mary Mann had still been alive in 1943 one might have been tempted to attribute that article to her.

We do not know whether Kate loved jewellery or had much of it — though she did lend a diamond bracelet to Elisabetta Marcantonio to wear on her wedding day. There are no rings or jewellery visible in the few images we have of her and it seems likely that Judy Harrison's jewels and ornaments are an invention to give 'Kitty' something valuable to steal. Certainly Kate's home contained valuable antique furniture and fine china,[3] but she didn't live in her father's 'gloomy old house' — Carlton Terrace was new when she moved in — though, of course, it may still have been gloomy. We do not know whether she had regular 'at homes' but she certainly hosted parties and invited friends to events to meet her protégés — just as Judy did.

100. Mary E. Mann (1848–1929), novelist and short story writer, Catherine Nichols' friend from their schooldays and authoress of 'The Eerie'.

The light-heartedness and generosity which Judy exhibits are not discernible in Kate's work or in her writing, but they are characteristics her friends recorded in their tributes to her. Similarly, the eclectic friendships and the frequent contact with the police when she found people ill-treating their animals also fit with what has been written about her. Her disregard for class and for her personal safety are themes that recur in her own stories of her adventures in Cornwall and abroad, though they are at odds with the persona she presented in interviews. In the story Judy is described as 'old' yet she can still run through the streets when she believes Cavassa is in danger. At the presentation of her portrait to the museum, Duleep Singh described his memory of Kate jumping out of a charabanc 'like a two year old' even though she had recently had a major operation and was over seventy, so it seems she, too, was physically energetic into old age.[4]

Alastor and Cavassa were both extremely good looking. Mary Mann did not think Alastor had any real powers — just the ability to observe — and that is what she gives Cavassa. But Kate and Mrs Pym both believed in Alastor absolutely, at least to begin with, and it is this open-mindedness, verging on gullibility, coupled with a desire for the mystical, that Mary Mann brings out in Judith.

Mary Mann had known Kate Nichols almost all her life and she was an unsparing observer. We believe it is fair to assume that Judy Harrison is an only slightly exaggerated representation of Kate. So here is the story in full. Perhaps it is the closest we shall ever get to a picture of Kate Nichols.

The Eerie

'I love people who can *do* things. Artists, musicians, actors, writers — such as these are always welcome at my house. I love *interesting* people. I don't care *what* they are — organ grinders out of the streets, tramps if you like. I had one delightful old man — a tramp — staying in my house for a month. Public schoolboy once — university man — *gone under*. The police made a fuss. What did I care? Let's fish them out when they go under, I say. Madmen? Oh, I don't draw the line even there. They call me half mad, myself. I'm *not*, mind you; or if I am, I'm glad I am. The wholly sane people are so stupid, so *afraid*. I'm not afraid of any one — nor am I afraid to amuse myself. What do *you* say?'

Thus Miss Judith Harrison — Judy, as she called herself, and liked to be called — explaining the idiosyncrasies of her temperament to the man who stood on the hearth beside her. She was never tired of explaining herself with both length and emphasis to anyone who would listen. Her friends, for their part, were accustomed to explain her with ease and brevity, in one word — a Crank.

She was lean, and old, and dark, with a face over which the feathered head-dress of the American Indian might have waved appropriately. It was nearly certain, if the fact had struck her, she would have adopted the ornament. Her garments had nothing to do with the prevailing fashion, but were chosen for some fancied artistic value. Her draperies were usually black, to match her hair, but always in hat, at throat, at waist, some touch of amber or vivid scarlet showed.

'I *love* colour. It is food and drink to me. Starve me if you like, but give me somewhere a dash of colour,' she said.

She lived in a large gloomy house where her father had lived before her, in a narrow old street of a cathedral city; and there, once a week, she was at home to any of her heterogeneous collection of friends who cared to visit her. Among them, because she was of good birth, rich, and in her odd way a lady always, came generally a sprinkling from the aristocratic county families. They never knew whom they might find there in the character of Star. An Italian with a hurdy-gurdy, singing in his native rags, a music-hall artist reciting in baggy, shabby dress clothes. Tonight it had been Cavassa.

There had been a crowd of the usual sort; gradually it had melted away and left her alone with him; Cavassa the seer, as he called himself. He had been giving an entertainment at the Assembly Rooms, and had come from there to Miss Harrison's At Home, at that lady's earnest solicitation.

'I *love* the mystic,' she had told him; but it was the beauty of his face, clear-cut and perfect as a piece of sculpture, which was his chief attraction for Judith Harrison — the beauty-lover, as she liked to be called.

He, naturally, had not desired to give the show away, or to make himself cheap in the town, where his performance was advertised for each night, from eight till ten, for a week to come. He had looked at the palm of a lady more than usually persistent, from whom he could not escape without rudeness, and had made a few enigmatical remarks on its lines which left her no wiser than before; he had gazed for a minute or two at the miniature of a soldier on a girl's white neck, and had given some, to her, satisfying minutiae of her brother's proceedings in India, at that moment. For the rest, he had lounged through the room with his languid air of graceful indifference, looking over the crowd with eyes that apparently did not see it, aloof, silent, and with the practised air of gloom and inscrutability, which was part of his stock-in-trade.

He stood now by the high, old-fashioned marble mantelpiece of the long drawing — room — worn, and shabby, and old like its mistress, yet filled with many valuable, and some beautiful things. At his feet sat Judy on the hearthrug, her skinny, jewelled hands clasped round her elevated knees, gazing up at him with eyes, once glorious, and still full of light.

'It's because you are so good to look at that I can't *bear* to let you go!' she told him. 'Never — *never* have I seen a man's face so perfect!'

He was not at all embarrassed, not visibly gratified. He was but a journeyman working at his trade, like another. The pale, chiselled face, the dark, gloomy eyes which seemed to see nothing till with an effort their gaze concentrated on a given object, when they saw more than most people's — these were but implements in his bag of tools.

'Tell me about yourself. Do tell me!' she besought him. 'When did you first discover this gift — this marvellous gift of second sight?'

He was disappointingly matter-of-fact in his reply.

'I discovered it when it was my only way of getting a living,' he said.

She nodded towards a mantelpiece crowded with ornaments. 'A crystal is there. Could you *really* read the future in it?'

He picked up the crystal, fingered it idly, and put it back again. 'I could — if it answered my purpose,' he said.

She nodded an enthusiastic head at him. 'I believe in the mystic with all my *soul*,' she told him. 'Yet I am not in the least clairvoyant. I believe in ghosts — oh, I should think I *do* believe in them! Yet never have I been permitted to see one. Isn't it *strange*?'

'Strange, indeed!' agreed Cavassa.

'It isn't as if I were just a Philistine. There's my housekeeper, now — oh, I ought to have thought of it before!' she said, suddenly breaking off. 'She *would* so like to see you. You wouldn't mind her coming in?'

'Not in the least, of course.'

'She's — what do you call it? — clairaudient. Is that it? Hears voices in the most wonderful way. Such wretches all my other housekeepers have turned out. This one is a *dear*. She would die for me. I like that, don't you?'

'It is useful,' Cavassa admitted; 'or it might be.'

'I was in a muddle for a housekeeper — I won't go to horrible registry offices, and so on; I wait for something to turn up — something always does if you wait — haven't you ever found it so? Suddenly this girl appeared. Said she'd been *drawn*.'

'How "drawn"?'

'Said I'd called her, and she'd come. Simply that. "You blessed creature," I said, "*come* along!" And she's been here ever since. My friend, ally, greatest earthly treasure, I call her.'

'And had you called her?'

'Spiritually, of course.'

She got up from her hearthrug, whisked her long draperies to the door.

'Kitty!' she called. 'Are the servants gone to bed, Kitty?'

'Yes, miss.'

'Can you come up, Kitty, or are you too tired? A gentleman is here who wants to see you.'

Kitty came with alacrity.

'Kitty and I often sit over the fire, and talk and smoke till it's time to get up in the morning,' Kitty's mistress informed the Seer, languidly listening, with his lack-lustre eyes, and gracefully indifferent air.

He looked at Kitty's plump figure in its tightly made dress and befrilled muslin apron. In it, and in her common, pale little face, with the upturned nose, the wide cheekbones, the pale, small eyes and snapping eyelids, was nothing arresting to the eyes of man. Cavassa looked at her, looked away, letting his eyes sweep round the room: looked at her again, again away; while her mistress, hugging her knees as she squatted on the hearthrug, told of Kitty's value as housekeeper, as friend, as intellectual companion.

When at length there came an instant's break in her volubility, and she looked up at him, she found Cavassa's eyes, steady, penetrating, focused at last on Kitty's face. Judith waited expectantly; he was going to give forth some interesting utterance now! She had thought he would be interested in Kitty, who was 'eerie', and had heard voices.

'Kitty loves the mystic — as I do,' the mistress explained encouragingly. 'You *do*, *don't* you, Kitty?'

'I love the eerie,' Kitty said.

'You have many beautiful things under your charge in this house,' was all Cavassa gave forth.

'There's a lot of silver and china to keep in order,' Kitty admitted with a little surprise.

'Better to spend your time in cleaning silver than in listening for voices,' he admonished.

It was very disappointing. Kitty blinked at him with her short-sighted, pale eyes, and laughed.

'Have you a man in the house?'

'No. We kept one till Kitty came. But they were more trouble than the women, weren't they, Kitty?'

'Indeed they were, miss. Thieves, and drunkards into the bargain.'

'And you have no fear of burglars?'

The women scorned the idea. Miss Harrison had friends among the worst characters in the city — the whole police force were her friends. Assuredly, they would not allow her to be harmed.

'Although I do say, Miss Harrison ought not to keep her jewellery in the house,' Kitty declared. 'It ought to be at the bank, I always tell her.'

'A lot of good it would do me there!' Miss Harrison scoffed. She put up brown fingers covered with flashing gems and fingered a diamond necklace she wore over a high black satin bodice. A bit of orange ribbon was pulled through her raven black hair, another width of it was tied round her dark-hued throat.

'Don't you *love* gems?' she enquired of Cavassa. 'I could look for hours into the glowing heart of a ruby. I *love* the flash and fire of these.'

Cavassa did not glance at the gems she touched. He had taken up, once again, the crystal from the mantelpiece, and stood there, idly shifting it with delicate fingertips. Presently, watching him, they saw that he was beginning to look into the crystal, holding it now half-hidden in his hollowed palms. His head came forward, the eyes which had been so listlessly indifferent were fixed with unswerving intentness on the sphere of glass he held.

'*Oh!*' said Judith Harrison, ecstatically expectant, and grasped the skirts of the other woman. 'Hush, Kitty! He is going to *tell* us something.'

A minute that seemed ten, before, with an utterance monotonous and difficult, like that of one who talks in his sleep, he began —

'I see a fire,' he said, 'a fire. And by it is a woman — a noble woman — gems at her breast and round her throat.'

'Oh!' breathed Judith again. 'Kitty — oh!' and put up a skinny hand to the diamonds sparkling on the black satin bust. 'Go on! *Do* go on!'

But another long, silent minute passed before the difficult voice began again.

'At the hearth,' it said, 'a something coiled — coil upon coil — which the woman in the jewels is tending.'

'My bicycle tyre, miss!' Kitty whispered enlighteningly to her mistress. 'I did have a trouble to get it on again today!'

'Almost lifeless — not quite,' went on the man with eyes glued on the crystal. 'A creeping, a creeping, a stealthy movement through the coils. A head is raised, a flat and cruel head — and from it there darts —'

'Oh! It isn't a snake. Do say it isn't a snake! I do hate them so,' Judith cried.

She scrambled to her knees and pulled appealingly on the tails of Cavassa's dress coat. 'I *am* so sorry!' she said 'but if anything in the world would make me have hysterics it would be *snakes*. You don't mind — *do* you — that I interrupted you?'

He replaced the crystal gently on the mantelpiece, and looked down without a smile at the strange figure of the woman kneeling beside him. Kitty, the housekeeper, had jumped up, pushing back her chair.

'Ugh! You've given us both the creeps,' she said with disgust.

Cavassa walked to the door. Judith, getting to her feet, stumbled across the room after him, wringing her hands entreatingly.

'Oh, *don't* go! *Don't* be angry. *Do* say it wasn't a snake!' she implored.

Cavassa bowed a ceremonious good-night. 'It was undoubtedly a bicycle tyre,' he said. His eyes rested for a space on the housekeeper opening the door for him. 'I had thought for a moment it might be a viper on the hearth,' he added as he passed her, and went out into the darkness.

Twelve o'clock of the next night found Miss Judith Harrison sitting alone over her dining-room fire, her feet on the fender, a cigarette between her lips. She had been spending the evening with some of the people with whom she foregathered. Two or three times a year she was asked to dine with a certain countess, who had a seat in the neighbourhood; but she accepted with equal alacrity an invitation to her bootmaker's, whose daughter had discovered a talent for painting.

The door opened, and the housekeeper appeared — appeared, and started back with a cry.

'Kitty! How white you look!'

Kitty closed the door behind her by falling back against it. 'And don't I feel white!' she said. She put her hands upon her heaving chest. 'My legs tremble under me; you gave me such a shock!' she explained. 'I thought you said you were out for the night, miss! I thought you were going to watch the stars, along with Mr Kingdon, through his telescope.'

'I said so. But Vincent Kingdon has a cold. His wife has put him to bed, instead. I would not stop in *her* stupid house if I might not be with Vincent. I came home half an hour ago. Didn't you hear me let myself in?'

Kitty had not heard, or her nerves would not have been in such a shaken condition at the sight of her mistress.

'You might have knocked me down with a feather,' Kitty declared. 'That comes of your having a latch-key, miss, and startling me out of my senses in this fashion.'

Miss Harrison laughed, and pointed, with one of her free, un-English gestures to the sideboard. 'Get yourself a glass of wine,' she said, 'and bring the cigarettes. I've smoked two since I came in, but I'll have another with you. Aren't the servants gone to bed?'

'Goodness, miss! Yes. Two hours ago!'

'But I heard voices in the kitchen as I crossed the hall.'

'Me, muttering to myself,' said Kitty at the sideboard.

'Didn't someone come up the stairs with you? I almost thought you shut someone outside the door.'

'Only me walking heavily, being so tired,' Kitty explained.

'Bring me a glass of port too, Kitty. We'll put our feet up on the fender and have a real good time. Now, *what* were you muttering to yourself about downstairs, you funny person?'

'When I feel eerie I talk to myself,' Kitty admitted. 'I've got a right-down eerie feeling tonight, miss.'

'Take care! You're spilling the wine. Your poor hand's shaking like a leaf, Kitty. Come on, child. Sit here.' She pulled up an arm-chair beside her own. 'Turn up your skirt — *do* — I know you like to turn up your skirt. I'll turn up mine too — look! — for company. *Now!* What's it like to feel eerie, you queer thing?'

Kitty, still very pale, shivered, and her teeth chattered. 'It's like that,' she said.

'Kitty!' the hand of the mistress clutched the housekeeper's knee. 'Is it how you felt that time when you heard my voice calling you? Is it?'

Kitty's pale eyes ceased to blink. She was silent for a minute, considering the question. 'That's it!' she said at length. 'That's just how I felt!' She began to shiver strongly. 'Oh, I hope, I *hope* I'm not going to hear any more voices!' she wailed.

'Don't be stupid!' Judith said. She looked with much interest at the young woman. Kitty and she worshipped the mystic — now they were going to have a demonstration. 'The voices will tell you something for your own good again!' she said encouragingly. 'They did before, you know. Why, we shouldn't have been *together*, child, but for the voices!'

Kitty was crying, the tears dropping down her cheeks.

'You haven't had a *bad* time, Kitty?'

'The best in the world,' Kitty declared — gulping, in her struggle with emotion.

'I know you *love* me, Kitty, and I love you, too. Remember that.'

'Yes. And even if that Cavassa with his crystal was to say different we would both know 'twas a lie.'

Judith threw up her hands ecstatically. '*What* a face!' she cried in reminiscent admiration. '*What* a sorrowful, soulful, haunting beauty! *There's* a man to suffer for, Kitty — to *die* for!'

'I believe you, miss,' agreed Kitty.

She sprang up suddenly from her chair, gave her mistress a wild look. 'Hark!' she cried.

The wine glass fell from her hand, shivered on the fender. 'Hark!' she whispered 'Hark!'

She turned round as if answering to a call, and looked towards the window. 'Don't you hear it?' she breathed. 'Plainly — quite plainly. Hark! Judith! Judith!'

'Calling *me*?' the owner of the name questioned in the still voice of awe. 'Who? *Whose* voice?'

'Cavassa's,' said Kitty, with fixed eyes. 'Calling on you — to save him.'

'Where? From what?' The mistress was on her feet in instant readiness.

'From death,' breathed the housekeeper.

'Where is he? Where can I find him? Does he say?'

'By the river. He has gone there — to drown himself.'

Rushing to where it hung on the back of a chair, Miss Harrison seized an ancient short opera-cloak of amber brocade with a dingy ermine fur, cast it about her shoulders, and pulled its hood over her wild, dark head.

'At once!' breathed Kitty, dreadfully staring at the window. 'The voice says "at once!"' Her own voice sank inaudibly over the last word and then shrieked it aloud. 'At once!' she screamed, and flung herself on her mistress. 'You shan't go! You shan't go!' she cried. 'Oh, my dear mistress, you shan't go!'

'Get out of my way,' said Judith fiercely, and flung her off.

The housekeeper fell on the floor and beat it wildly with her hands.

'Not alone! Not alone, dear mistress! Take me!'

'A lot of use you'll be to me in that state!' the mistress cried, and would have spurned her from her path. 'Don't be a *fool*, Kitty!'

But the young woman clung with both hands to the trailing black satin skirt. 'Not in your jewels, miss,' she cried. "'Tisn't safe, I tell you — not safe, this time of night, and you out, unprotected. Take them off, miss, take them off!'

At such a crisis Judith herself could have scorned such mean considerations, but the grasp on her skirts was not to be shaken off.

'Fool! *Fool*, to stop me!' she cried; but unfastened at the same time the diamond necklace from her throat, wrenched off the bracelets from her arms — they hung loosely on the lean wrists and needed no unfastening — and flung them at the woman on the floor.

'Your brooch!' panted Kitty.

And the brooch, torn from its place in the amber ribbon at the throat, was also dashed on the carpet.

'Now!' cried the mistress, 'Remember, a man's life is at stake. Do not dare to stop me for another moment.'

Kitty, laughing and crying in loud hysterics, released her clutch on the skirts, to beat her hands again on the carpet.

With a wild leap over the prostrate body, with a swishing and whisking of her skirts through the door, Judith was gone.

The skies were alight with the stars she was to have watched from Vincent Kingdon's observatory, but if they had been black as her own coarse hair, no fear would Judith Harrison have felt. She experienced a certain awe of the unknown, into which she had nevertheless such a curiosity to pry, but terror of man or beast she was incapable of knowing.

The streets were deserted at that hour, save that here and there a policeman walked his beat. He would turn and look after the hurrying tall figure in the ermine-trimmed opera cloak, with scarce a touch of surprise. To all the members of the force, Judith, bent on all sorts of strange errands, was familiar.

One had called at her house to warn her of the dangerous character of the tramp to whom she was giving shelter. He had been sent forth flying, with no word of thanks. Another had arrived in the nick of time to rescue her from a man with whom she was *fighting* in one of the worst slums of the city. She had interposed in a quarrel between husband and wife — with this result. A score of them had, at different times, been forced by her, wildly gesticulating and raging in the streets, to take names and addresses of owners of horses unfit to be driven, to rescue dogs from masters who insufficiently fed them, cats who were ill-used. To the wives and children of the local force she was to give a tea and a Christmas tree in the big Assembly Room next week.

Each man looked at her as she passed, therefore, said a respectful 'Good-night, Miss,' and took no further notice.

She went as quickly as her legs would carry her, taking a short cut to the river. It led her, in the first instance, through the principal streets of the town; then through a short alley and a long lane of houses, where no woman respecting herself would have walked even in daylight. It took her, again for a short distance, down a wide street, once the aristocratic quarter of the city, with houses almost palatial in size on each side. Arrived here, she would still have her way to make through the least desirable part of her journey, by long, dark, noisome ways infested with the scum of the city; after which, the river.

So far she had not paused an instant on her course, and for the most part she had taken it at a run. Half-way down the broad street she became aware of steps going on ahead, ringing on the pavement, echoing clearly in the frosty air. She made out the figure of a man moving before her leisurely; her nostrils caught the fragrance of the cigar he smoked. A minute and she had overtaken him, passed him, having caught at a glance as she did so the long oval of a white cheek. She came to a dead stop, turned, and clutched him by his coat sleeves.

'Cavassa!'

They stood together in the silence and emptiness, he peering into her face.

'Miss Harrison, isn't it? What a time of night!'

'*What* are you doing with yourself? *Where* are you going?'

He felt the bony fingers dig into his arms. 'I have been earning an extra five guineas by amusing a party of fools in one of these houses, after my own performance. I am going to the river.'

'I *knew* it. I have come to stop you.' The fingers were like iron clamps about his arms. 'You must come with me.'

'I think not, Miss Harrison. Won't you, on the contrary, come with me? You are fond of beautiful things. Come and see the reflection of the stars in the water.'

'Not I. Not a step. It is fatal. You shall not move another step nearer the river. I will stand here, clinging to you, all night. If you attempt to escape I will *scream*.'

'I fancy I could silence your screaming. Why should you scream?'

'You are going to make away with yourself! To *drown!*'

'I? I don't think so. I told you I am going to look at the reflection of the stars in the river. After a double performance, as I've had tonight, I don't sleep very well; I'm on edge. The river calms me.'

'You shall never reach it — *never*, unless you drag me with you. Unless you drown me too, you shall not kill yourself. You would not drown an old woman? I do not look one. I look as I did twenty years ago — that is because my hair is black and my heart is young. But I'm old, really. *Quite* old. You would not drown an old woman, Cavassa. *Quite* an old woman — and I have run all the way.'

Her dark Indian-looking face was pale in the starlight, her eyes blazed with the intensity of her purpose, her ermine-trimmed hood had fallen backwards, strands of her black hair were blown across her face. In her trailing satin skirt, and her short, tawdry opera-cloak, she was a grotesque figure.

'How did you know I should be here?' he asked her.

'The voices,' she explained. 'Kitty, my housekeeper, you know, — she heard you call. Clairaudient — you remember? You called my name, "Judith! Judith!" I came at once. You can't deny the voices. O, turn back, and *let* me save you!'

'Supposing I had been going to drown myself, which I was not going to do, why should you care so much?' he asked, with the slow melancholy which to his audience was so attractive.

'*Care?* Do you think I am of stone, Cavassa, that I should not care? Your youth, your manhood to be thrown away! Your beautiful, *beautiful* face to be disfigured in the black mud of our dirty river! You don't know, perhaps, how people *look* when they're drowned — you'd never think of getting out of it *that* way if you did. I do know. I went and looked at the body of a friend of mine who had gone to the river rather than to prison. He came and told me it was all up — what he had done — that his children would be disgraced. "Go and *drown* yourself," I told him. He went. Afterwards — when I saw him — I wished I had given him other advice.'

'And while you rushed, at her bidding, unprotected through the night, is Kitty — the housekeeper you so prize — left in charge of all the beautiful treasures of your house?'

'Kitty? There's *no-one* I trust like Kitty!'

'That cabinet full of old snuff-boxes; the miniatures set in jewels on your walls; that exquisite Sevres vase on your chimney-piece?'

Judith laughed, clinging to the young man's arm. 'All the old rubbish of many generations!' she said. 'She's got my diamonds, too, from my neck; my *bracelets*, my *brooches*. She thinks a great deal more of them than I do. She *made* me take them off, for fear some-one should rob me. I was so angry with her — *poor* Kitty! — I nearly knocked her down. I remember she lay screaming on the floor, and I leapt over her body —'

'We will go to your home, Miss Harrison, as quickly as we can; and I think we will take a policeman with us,' Cavassa said.

In the end they took two — which was a good thing. For, while one took charge of Kitty, as she came quickly and furtively round the corner of the street in which Miss Harrison lived, her mistress's jewel-case in her hand, the other gave chase to the man who scooted, flinging his booty to right and left as he ran down the road. He was the 'eerie' Kitty's husband as well as her accomplice, it turned out, a character already well known to the police.

Judy Harrison was less upset by the discovery of her housekeeper's baseness than might have been imagined. It was not the first time by a great many she had trusted and been deceived. It was certain not to be the last. She was, however, too unhinged to go to bed that night, she protested. She and Cavassa made up a roaring fire in the dining room, foraged the larder and cellar in search of food and drink of which both stood in need. She made him sit in the most comfortable chair on the hearth, while she squatted, embracing her knees, on the rug opposite him, gazing at leisure, and to her heart's content, at the beauty of his face.

So they made what Miss Harrison called 'a night of it.'

Once or twice she stretched out her lean hand and tapped his knee to emphasise her words and her satisfaction.

'After all, you *were* going to the river!' she reminded him. 'There *was* something eerie about it after all, Cavassa! I *love* the eerie!' she said.

We do not know whether Kate Nichols ever read her friend's story — or whether their friendship survived the publication.

Kate Nichols died on 30th January 1923, of a cancer. She had been operated on two years previously, but the operation had not removed the tumour and simply delayed the inevitable end by a matter of months. She left just £89 5s 10d having given away most of her money before she died. She also left mementos 'either pictures or trinkets or otherwise' as her brother Frederick, acting as her executor, 'in his absolute and sole discretion may see fit' to a handful of friends (Mary Thorn, Beatrix Simonds, Catherine Green, Elizabeth Capaldi [sic] and Miss Oxley) — and family (her brother Alfred, cousin Constance Banister and her sister Alice's children). Presumably she had given something to Frederick and his family during her lifetime.

Kate's real memorial is her work. She was not a great artist, but she was a good one, and she deserves to be much, much better known.

*101. Catherine Maude Nichols
as an old lady.*

Notes

Unless otherwise stated, information in this book comes from standard local and family history sources — parish records, birth, marriage and death certificates, census returns, trade directories etc.

NCM = Norwich Castle Museum
NML = Norwich Millennium Library
NRO = Norfolk Record Office

Chapter 1

1 NRO MC2716 Mann collection, uncatalogued.
2 NRO MC2577/7/23, 985X1 Lilly S. Jackson's memoir.
3 NRO MC2716 Mann collection. Bertie's diaries and Mary Mann's letters to Tom Ordish.
4 *Eastern Evening News*, 4th September 1939.
5 *Bucks Herald*, 25th July 1908.
6 *Western Morning News*, 24th July 1922.
7 She was, apparently, often taken advantage of — see, for example NRO MC2716 letters in the Mann collection; 'The Eerie'; *Eastern Daily Press*, 22nd February 1943 — 'Of course she was often deceived and imposed upon: her belief in mankind was too generous to escape from such misfortune'.

Chapter 2

1 Gladys Engel Lang and Kurt Lang, *Etched in Memory: the building and survival of artistic reputation* (Chapel Hill: University of North Carolina Press, 1990). Unfortunately, the Langs do not reference much of their information.
2 NRO MC 2716, Mann collection.
3 *The Women's Penny Paper*, July 1889.
4 Will of William Peter Nichols.
5 NRO MS11322/831.
6 NRO MS11322/1041.
7 See, for example NRO MS11322/1044.

8 Op. cit.
9 'HSS' in *Eastern Daily Press*, 22nd February 1943.

Chapter 3

1 H. W. Saunders, *A History of the Norwich Grammar School*, Jarrold, 1932.
2 There are a number of works by him in Norwich Castle Museum – the overall accession number for the collection is NWHCM 1954.138.
3 Roy Porter, *The Greatest Benefit to Mankind: a medical history of humanity from antiquity to the present*, HarperCollins, 1997.
4 Peter Eade, *The Norfolk and Norwich Hospital 1770 to 1900*, Jarrold, 1900.
5 1855–1941, surgeon and medical historian.
6 A. Batty Shaw, 'The Norwich School of Lithotomy' in *Medical History*, 14 (03) pp.221–259.
7 ibid.
8 Irvine Loudin, *Medical Care and the General Practitioner*, OUP, 1986, p. 111.
9 *Norfolk News*, 23rd July 1870.
10 NRO MC279/6,679X1.
11 Numerous newspaper reports December 1861–January 1862; *The Great Lunacy Case of Mr. W. F. Windham*, Vickers, 1862.
12 For example, *Norfolk Chronicle*, 14th April 1849; *Salisbury and Winchester Journal*, 24th April 1869; *Norfolk News*, 12th September 1846.
13 For example *Norfolk Chronicle*, 21st April 1866.
14 *Norfolk News*, 16th July 1870.
15 *Norfolk News*, 3rd November 1866. Some sources say Kate presented a bouquet of roses to the Princess, but the roses were actually in a basket by a tree the Princess planted. This misinformation first appears in Duleep Singh's speech when a portrait of Kate was presented to Norwich Museum and is repeated in several sources. The newspaper gives an almost minute-by-minute account of the visit and it is clear that what Kate presented was an album.
16 For example *Norfolk Chronicle*, 2nd December 1854.
17 NRO MC279/6,679X1.
18 Norwich Castle Museum NWCHM2008.128.13:F.
19 www.findagrave.com/cgi-bin/fg.cgi?page=gr&GRid=71205979.
20 *Eastern Daily Press*, 20th April 1925.
21 *Crockford's Clerical Directory*.
22 Roll of Honour 1914–18 www.diaagency.ca/railways/Casualties.htm.
23 www.druidry.org.

Chapter 4

1 See Chapter 9, for example.
2 *Glasgow Herald*, 10th March 1892.
3 *Norfolk Chronicle*, 26th January 1856.
4 Mary E. Mann, *Gran ma's Jane*, Methuen, 1903.
5 NRO Mann collection MC2716. At the time of writing this collection is uncatalogued so it is impossible to give more precise references.
6 All the letters quoted are in NRO MC2716.

7   'HSS' in the *Eastern Daily Press*, 22nd February 1943.
8   Joan Banger's notes from documents destroyed by the library fire of 1994. Norwich Millennium Library.
9   *Norwich Mercury*, September 1852
10 Joan Banger, op. cit.
11 Marjorie Allthorpe-Guyton and John Stevens, *A Happy Eye: a School of Art in Norwich 1845–1982*, Jarrold, 1982.
12 NRO MC2577/7/23, 985X1 Lilly Jackson's Memoir.
13 NRO ETN3/4/, press cuttings books.
14 *Norfolk Chronicle*, 28th April 1821.
15 Sydney Kitson, *The Life of John Sell Cotman*, Faber and Faber, 1937.
16 Report to the House of Commons, 6th August 1850, Reports and Documents related to the heads of Provincial Schools of Art and Design.
17 Trevelyan MSS, University Library, Newcastle-upon-Tyne.
18 NRO NCR case 27a, Norwich School of Art collections.
19 *Eastern Daily Press*, 3rd October 1891.
20 NCM 1979. A letter from Katherine Havers, daughter of Ethel Buckingham.
21 *Architect Exuberant: George Skipper*. David Jolley Exhibition Catalogue December 1975.
22 Norwich Castle Museum NWCHM 1969.557:F.
23 Joan Banger, op. cit. It is not clear where this quotation comes from as the notes are not entirely reliable when it comes to sources.

Chapter 5

Most of the information in this chapter comes from one of two sources — visits to the Leicester Print Workshop and discussions with students, and Bamber Gascoigne, *How to Identify Prints*, Thames & Hudson 1986.

1   We have been unable to identify D. Hume.
2   E.g. *The Bookman* 1913, *Women's Penny Paper* 1889.
3   Hand-made lithographs such as Kate produced should not be confused with offset lithography, a commercial process.

Chapter 6

Unless otherwise stated, information about the Norwich School of Art comes from Marjorie Allthorpe-Guyton and John Stevens, *A Happy Eye: a School of Art in Norwich 1845–1982*, Jarrold, 1982. Information about the Royal Society of Painter-Etchers comes from Martin Hopkinson, *No Day without a Line: the History of the Royal Society of Painter-Printmakers 1880–1999*, Oxford: Ashmolean Museum, 1999.

1   J. Johnson and A. Greutzner, *The Dictionary of British Artists 1880–1940*, Woodbridge: Antique Collectors' Club, 1976.
2   Algernon Graves, *The Royal Academy of Arts: a complete dictionary of contributors and their work from its foundation in 1769 to 1904*, George Bell, 1905–06.
3   31st May 1892.
4   NRO MS11322.
5   July 1889.

6   Graves, op. cit.
7   NRO MC2577/7/23, 985XI Lilly Bull's memoir.
8   www.penleehouse.org.uk/newlyn-school.html.
9   Lilly Bull, op. cit.
10 ibid.
11 Unidentified press cutting in Norwich Millennium Library, filed under 'Nichols, C. M.'
12 *Norwich Chronicle*, 21st January 1899. It is just possible that the engraving 'Fire and Water' that she submitted to the Norwich Art Circle Black and White exhibition showed the timber yard ablaze.
13 It is not our intention here to give an overview of the Norwich School of painters, but for further information see, for example, Giorgia Bottinelli, *A Vision of England*, Norwich Castle Museum, 2013 or visit the Norfolk Museums website www.norfolkmuseumscollections.org to view images of their work.
14 Norwich Castle Museum NWHCM L 1967.9.1948 and NWHCM L 1967.9.92.
15 Ashmolean Museum, Oxford WA1950.178.134.
16 C. M. Nichols, *Musings at Cromer* and *Lines of Thought*, Norwich: Jarrold, 1887 and 1892.
17 Martin Hopkinson, *No Day without a Line: the History of the Royal Society of Painter-Printmakers 1880–1999*, Oxford: Ashmolean Museum, 1999.
18 *Norwich Argus*, 15th September 1885.
19 1881 census. The boarding house was at 41 Devonshire Street, Marylebone.
20 Minutes of the Council meeting in May 1881.
21 The collection can be viewed awww.uwe.ac.uk/sca/research/cfpr/dissemination/archives/pdf_archives/PP1880-1909reduced.pdf

Chapter 7

Much of the information and many of the pictures in this chapter come from *The Great Gothic Fane* (author unknown) published by Heath, Cranton and Ousley Ltd, London, 1913, and *The Third National Catholic Congress*, published by Effingham House, London, 1912. We are also indebted to Stephen Slack and the Archive of St John's Cathedral, Norwich, for information about Catholicism in Norwich in Kate Nichols' day and for details of the baptism ceremony.

1   In the Cathedral archive. The words 'sub conditione' indicate a 'conditional' baptism: the Roman Catholic church did not admit that Anglican rites were necessarily valid, because nobody could be sure they had been performed correctly.
2   Andrew Stephenson, *The Maddermarket Theatre, Norwich*, Norwich: Norwich Players, 1971.
3   Information from Stephen Slack quoting Brother Ninian Arbuckle, Archivist of the UK Franciscan Order.
4   Marjorie Allthorpe-Guyton and John Stevens, *A Happy Eye: a School of Art in Norwich 1845–1982*, Jarrold, 1982, p. 35.
5   Mary E. Mann, *The Parish of Hilby*, 1883, republished ISIS, 2007, p. 336.
6   NFK/QC ZZ8Z *Catholicism For and Against*, a bound copy of Catholic pamphlets from the J. J. Colman Library – now in the Local Studies section of Norwich Millennium Library. It includes C. M. Nichols, *A Few Words about the Catholic Faith*, 1885.
7   ibid.
8   *The Great Gothic Fane*, footnote on p. 66.

9 Published by Effingham House, London, 1912.

10 p. 250. St Walstan was a Norfolk man, the son of a wealthy gentry family in Bawburgh, but in his youth he decided to eschew his family's wealth and spend his days labouring with the poor. At the age of seven Walstan received instruction from Bishop Theodred of Elmham. When he was only 12 he left his parents' home and travelled to Taverham in Norfolk where he worked as a farm labourer. Walstan soon gained a reputation for hard work and piety and also developed an affinity with the poor and was charitable in the extreme, giving both his food and clothing to those less fortunate than himself. It is said that Walstan was so charitable that he sometimes even gave his shoes away, going barefoot himself. He applied himself to the meanest and most painful labour in a perfect spirit of penance and humility; fasted much, and spent time in fervent prayer. He made a vow of celibacy, but never became a monk. He died on 30th May 1016 at work in a meadow after seeing a vision of an angel while cutting hay. His body was laid on a cart pulled by two white oxen as he had instructed, and the cortège ended up at Bawburgh, where he was buried. At the three points along the journey where the oxen stopped, springs appeared (though only the well at Bawburgh can now be found) and the water in them was found to have miraculous curative properties.

Chapter 8

1 NRO MC2577/7/23 985x1 Lilly Bull's memoir.

2 Lilly says she gave it to him free.

3 Parts of Lilly's memoir mirror exactly the obituary in the *Eastern Daily Press*, 31st January 1923. It may be that Lilly copied parts of it out — or it may be that she or Mrs Pym wrote the original.

4 NRO MC109/104-7 573x4.

5 'HSS' in the *Eastern Daily Press*, 2nd February 1943.

6 NRO MC109/104-7 573x4 and MS11322/1045.

7 NRO MC109/104-7 573x4.

8 Christy Campbell, *The Maharajah's Box: an imperial story of conspiracy, love and a guru's prophecy*, HarperCollins, 2000.

9 www.temiskamingartgallery.ca/ernest-sawford-dye/.

10 NRO MC2716 Bertie Mann's diary.

Chapter 9

Unless otherwise stated, the information in this chapter comes from Adrienne May and Brian Watts, *Wide Skies: a century of painting and painters in Norfolk*, Tiverton: Halsgrove, 2003.

1 84 in 1887, for example.

2 All the information about members and their exhibits comes from the catalogues of the Norwich Art Circle 1885–1900 which are held at NRO ETN 11/3.1 and the Norwich Art Circle catalogues 1900–23 which are held at the Castle Museum, Norwich, and from the Circle's papers NRO BOL 6/18, 742X6.

Chapter 11

1 Souvenir of the George Borrow Celebrations, Norwich, July 1913.

2 NRO MS11322/189.

3 NRO MC2577/7/23 985x1, Lilly Bull's memoir.
4 George A. Stephens, *Borrow House Museum*, Norwich Public Library, 1927.
5 Souvenir op. cit.
6 NRO MS11322/768, Catalogue of the George Borrow exhibition at the museum.
7 Stephens, op. cit.
8 NRO MS11322.
9 NRO MS11322/831.
10 NRO MS11322/123.
11 Unidentified press cutting in Norwich Millennium Library, filed under 'Nichols, C. M.'
12 'Girl Students in the London Art Schools', *Girls' Realm*, April 1889.
13 NRO MS11322/1044. Advertising hand-out.
14 Joan Banger's notes. A catalogue of the exhibition in the Colman and Rye collection in Norwich was destroyed in the library fire of 1994.
15 NRO MS11322/1044, op. cit.

Chapter 12

1 Most of the information in this chapter comes from the article 'Lovely Liz' in the *Eastern Daily Press*, 2nd December 1949, and from documents supplied by Maddie Bartle who is one of Elisabetta's descendants.
2 E.g. John E. Zucchi, *Little Slaves of the Harp: Italian Child Street Musicians in Paris*, Liverpool University Press, 1999. Despite the title, Zucchi deals with child musicians in London and New York as well as Paris.

Chapter 13

1 'HSS' in the *Eastern Daily Press*, 2nd February 1943.
2 NRO MC2716, Mann collection.
3 Mary E. Mann, *Rose at Honeypot*, 1906; *Astray in Arcady*, 1910.
4 Norwich Millennium Library RSPCA papers.
5 See Chapter 14.
6 en.wikipedia.org/wiki/The_Blue_Cross.
7 *Bucks Herald*, 25th July 1908.
8 Leicestershire Record Office, 23D57.
9 http://archive.org/details/revolutionaryrevooimme.
10 'Queen of the Pheasants' appears in *Men and Dreams*, 1912; 'Blazing away at the Birds' is in *Through the Window*, 1913.
11 en.wikipedia.org/wiki/Frances_Power_Cobbe.
12 Norwich Millennium Library ref. 034676289.
13 en.wikipedia.org/wiki/Cruelty_to_Animals_Act_1876.
14 NRO HMN 5/237/1–37, HMN 5/238/1–27 738x3.
15 www.brown-dog/about/brown-dog-affair/.
16 *Cox's Who's Who in Norfolk and Suffolk*, London 1912.
17 en.wikipedia.org/wiki/British_Union_for_the_Abolition_of_Vivisection.
18 1st February 1923.

Chapter 14

1 See Marion Aldis and Pam Inder, *MEM: a biography of Mary E. Mann, Norfolk novelist 1848–1929*, Dereham: Larks Press, 2013. In 1910 a 'Dr B' — probably Dr Bussell, Rector of Mundford — threatened a libel action against her because he believed a character was based on him.

2 'HSS' in the *Eastern Daily Press*, 22nd February 1943.

3 Sale catalogue February 1923, Norwich Castle Museum.

4 Unidentified press cutting 'Portrait for the Castle Museum' filed under 'Nichols, C. M.' in the collection in the Millennium Library, Norwich.

Index

All numbers are page numbers, not illustration numbers.
Numbers in **bold type** indicate the presence of an illustration.